The Book of Egyptian Ritual

Simple Rites and Blessings for Everyday

JOCELYN ALMOND AND KEITH SEDDON

Thorsons

Thorsons
An Imprint of HarperCollins*Publishers*
77–85 Fulham Palace Road,
Hammersmith, London W6 8JB

The Thorsons website address is:
www.thorsons.com

and *Thorsons*
are trademarks of
HarperCollins*Publishers* Limited

First published as *An Egyptian Book of Shadows* by Thorsons 1999
This edition 2002

1 3 5 7 9 10 8 6 4 2

A catalogue record for this book
is available from the British Library

ISBN 0 00 713287 5

Printed in Great Britain by
Martins the Printers, Berwick upon Tweed

Contents

Acknowledgements

The authors are very grateful to the following publishers for their kind cooperation in granting permission for the use of extracts from their publications to compose the rites in this book.

Aris & Phillips for extensive extracts from *The Ancient Egyptian Pyramid Texts* (1969) by RO Faulkner, and *The Ancient Egyptian Coffin Texts* (3 volumes) (1973) by RO Faulkner.

Oxford University Press for extensive extracts from *The Ancient Egyptian Pyramid Texts* (1969) by RO Faulkner. Copyright © Oxford University Press (1969), by permission of Oxford University Press.

Thames & Hudson for extracts from *Myth and Symbolism in Ancient Egypt* (1959) by RT Rundle Clark, and *Egyptian Mysteries: New Light on Ancient Knowledge* (1981) by Lucie Lamy.

Extracts from the following works have also been included.

The Book of the Dead by EA Wallis Budge (1989), Arcana.

Egyptian Religion by EA Wallis Budge (1997), Citadel Press.

The Gods of the Egyptians (2 volumes) by EA Wallis Budge (1969),
    Dover Books.

The Myth of the Goddess by Anne Baring and Jules Cashford (1991),
    'Hymn to Nut', pages 259–60, Viking. Copyright © Anne Baring
    and Jules Cashford, 1991.

Ancient Egyptian Literature (volume 1 of 3) by Miriam Lichtheim
    (1975), 'Hymn to Min', page 204, University of California Press.
    Copyright © Regents of the University of California, 1973–1980.

The authors have made all reasonable effort to contact the copyright
holders of all the material used to request permission for its inclusion
in this book. If through error or omission any copyright holders have
not been contacted, the publishers would be very pleased to hear
from them so that appropriate acknowledgements may be included
in future editions.

The authors would like to thank the following for their permission
to reproduce copyright material in the colour plate section.

Four Sons of Horus. © The Ancient Egypt Picture Library.

Opening of the Mouth ceremony. © E Strouhal/Werner Forman
    Archive.

Horus of Edfu. © Werner Forman Archive.

Foreword

by Olivia Robertson, Archpriestess and Co-founder of the Fellowship of Isis

This brilliant and scholarly work has long been needed to fill a gap for all those of us who use Egyptian religion for ceremonial and magical practices. For too long those who seek to gain the beauty, nobility and wisdom of ancient Egypt have been presented with a mixture of Qabalah, theosophy and Celtic ways which, admirable as these are, have no links with Egypt! For instance, in the Western Mystery schools, 'sun' is equated with male: 'moon' with female – with all the Patriarchal connotations this suggests. But the Sky Goddess of our whole galaxy was – indeed is – the Goddess Nuit. The moon was ruled by the God Khonsu. The geometrical, hierarchical ideas of the Middle East with emphasis on formulae and the written word do not blend with the pictorial, right-side-of-the-brain magic of Egypt. The Middle East, especially Qabalah, speaks to us through sound. 'In the Beginning was the Word.' But the whole hidden enigma of Egypt is concealed yet openly expressed in Sphinx and pyramid and in the processional journey of life and lives beyond, painted in temple and tomb. So it is excellent to have the more ancient Pyramid Texts used in this book, which have been too long neglected in favour of the more popularized *Book of the Dead* or *Coming Forth by Day*.

The authors are well qualified to set themselves the formidable task of presenting the mighty liturgy and ways of ancient Egypt adapted for practical use for modern followers of this ancient Way.

I myself am acquainted with the dedication, imagination and love of Egypt shown by Jocelyn Almond, PhD. She is a most successful Priestess-Hierophant of the College of Isis, the scholarly side of the Fellowship of Isis, and runs her own Magi Degree Course. She is a correspondence tutor for Fairfax University, USA.

Keith Seddon, PhD, was Editor of *The Philosopher* and Associate Lecturer at the University of Hertfordshire. Jocelyn and Keith have published two books on the Tarot. They have also written works on their own, Jocelyn in Pagan magazines, and Keith in publications dealing with philosophy and the humanities.

The format of the book involves rites entirely of ancient Egyptian origin that can be used, by as few as four people at home, for the eight Pagan seasonal rites of the solstices, equinoxes and cross-quarter days. However, the book provides much deeper infor-mation than simply attractive and beautiful ceremonies. Readers are presented with information on the religious and magical beliefs of the ancient Egyptians, their concepts of the Neteru, the Deities, and the all-important reality of the Deities presiding. To give an exam-ple: the rite of the Summer Solstice involves a Goddess who is being worshipped more than ever in our age – the lion Goddess of the Sun, Sekhmet. Her myth, so relevant to our dangerous times, describes the destruction of much of the human race, until the righteous anger of Sekhmet – the Life Force – is pacified by a return to truth and justice.

The very ancient and the very new are presented in what should prove a valuable sourcebook for those who are involved in the ancient Egyptian revival in New Aeon form.

Olivia Robertson
Archpriestess and Co-Founder of the Fellowship of Isis
Clonegal Castle
Enniscorthy
Eire

Egyptian Paganism

Egyptian civilization is extraordinarily ancient. The *Pyramid Texts*, which are the oldest religious writings in the world and which are carved on the walls of five pyramids at Saqqara in Lower Egypt, have been dated to 2350 BC, yet the culture which produced these texts and built these pyramids was already highly developed and sophisticated at that time. Recent research by the geologist Professor Robert Schock, as reported by Robert Bauval and Graham Hancock in their book *Keeper of Genesis* (Mandarin, 1997), suggests that, at a conservative estimate, based on evidence of rain erosion, the Great Sphinx at Giza could date from between 7000 and 5000 BC when there was heavy rainfall in Egypt. After that time, such erosion could not have occurred, for the climate changed. Many geologists agree with this assessment which, if true, would make Egyptian civilization at least twice as old as current archeological orthodoxy will allow – a conclusion so startling as to be almost eerie.

As we gaze back in our imaginations across this vast gulf of time, Egyptian culture may seem strange to us. At first sight it has an alien, even alienating, atmosphere about it, to the extent that some people have looked for literally alien, extraterrestrial influences to explain what otherwise seems so weird as to be inexplicable. The images which survive from tombs and temples, of pharaohs, queens and the mighty gods, seem aloof, haughty, impassive, in their formal, stylized poses. In spectacular wall paintings, some of which have survived for millennia with their brilliant colours intact, these elegant figures stand in profile in ordered ranks, their peculiar sidelong gaze never meeting ours, as they perform for eternity the sacred rites of succouring the justified dead. In massive statuary the gods and pharaohs sit in perfect repose, inscrutable expressions on their utterly serene faces. Such images are awe-inspiring, but scarcely approachable. The animal-headed deities with human bodies are even more baffling: perhaps to some eyes they seem sinister, menacing – a curiously primitive remnant of prehistoric tribal cults persisting into a civilized age. Even the Greeks who were their contemporaries found this aspect of the Egyptians' religion quite grotesque and rather despicable. Our own culture's fictional portrayal of ancient Egyptian beliefs and practices focusing on horrible curses, black magic, mummies revived from the dead, and arcane rites involving human sacrifice, hardly shows the religion in a favourable light.

In spite of all this, ancient Egypt holds an undeniable fascination for many people: its mystery, its strangeness, is an intrinsic part of its appeal. We glimpse something that we do not understand, and we feel drawn to look and look again and to keep on looking, and gradually we see more, and understand more of what we are seeing. Eventually it will not seem strange at all, but very familiar; for the truth of the matter is that ancient Egypt is neither alien nor alienating: it is the culture behind our own culture and the civilization from which our own civilization grew. We tend to think of our culture as having descended from that of Greece and Rome, for down the centuries an emphasis on classical education has reinforced this view: but behind the glory of Greece there flourished another civilization from which the Greeks themselves claimed to have derived their learning, and compared with which they saw themselves to be like children – and that civilization was Egypt.

Religion in Egyptian Society

The culture of ancient Egypt was profoundly religious, but it was not religious in the sense by which we understand it in our secular society today. One of the names for the country itself was *ta neteru*, 'land of the gods', reflecting the fact that religion in ancient Egypt was all-pervasive to the extent that they did not even have a word for it. Religion and spirituality were intrinsic to absolutely everything that the ancient Egyptians did. Since a word has a meaning only if it may be applied to some things to distinguish them from others, a word which applies to absolutely everything could have no use. So, for the ancient Egyptians, it was taken for granted that everything was of spiritual and religious significance. The gods were everywhere, in everything, influencing everything. For the Egyptians, too, spirituality and religion were totally inseparable from magic, and for this they did have a word, and the word was *heka*. *Heka* is a spiritual force within the universe, but also a god in its own right, or, to use the Egyptian word, it was a *neter* – a divine principle.

Egyptian religion was above all a Pagan religion – it was a religion of nature. Nowadays there is a tendency to think of Paganism as a rustic tradition of old folk customs handed down by word of mouth, largely because this is the form in which remnants of it have survived. In the Pagan revival which is taking place in Britain and the USA today, the predominance of Wicca or witchcraft tends to confirm this view. We should not forget, however, that ancient Rome, with its urbanized culture of centrally-heated housing and public baths, was as much a Pagan civilization as was ancient Greece, with its more pastoral, idyllic image. North European Shamanism is no more Pagan just because it has rustic charm than is the religion of ancient Egypt practised with great ceremony by state officials in magnificent temples, the building of which is a feat that in some cases still defies modern engineering techniques. Some commentators, extolling the sophistication and subtlety of certain aspects of ancient Egyptian religion, have tried to find in it a prefiguring of Christianity, with a parallel between Jesus Christ and Osiris. Be this as it may, Egyptian religion is Pagan through and through; but this does not mean that it is necessarily either crude or rustic, for any such view of Paganism is a misconception.

Because of the allure of Egypt, many modern Pagans are now turning there for a spiritual focus, reviving the worship of the ancient deities – the *neteru*, the divine principles manifesting in nature. What they find, if they know how to enter the Inner Planes (or the *Neterkhert*, as the Egyptians called this psychic-spiritual realm) are not weird, alien, unapproachable entities, but vibrant, living beings, the archetypes of the collective unconscious, to use a Jungian term. For yes, it is true: the *neteru* are alive today – they are living in our very souls, they are part of our innermost being, and they can even today be our intimate companions, if we only know how to reach them.

Egyptian Religious Texts and the Role of Magic

So where does one begin in contacting these mighty entities? Sadly, there is very little material available at the present time to assist the modern Pagan who wishes to conduct authentic rituals for invoking the Egyptian gods. That is why we have written this much-needed book, to help other Pagans who seek communion with Deity in an Egyptian mode. The rites in this book have been composed entirely from translations of ancient Egyptian texts – chiefly the *Pyramid Texts*, the *Coffin Texts*, and the *Book of the Dead*. The oldest of these sources, the *Pyramid Texts*, as already explained, dates from 2350 BC, and the *Book of the Dead* was compiled about 1000 years later, while the *Coffin Texts* are an intermediate version of similar material embellishing sarcophagi from the early second millennium BC. We have used the famous translation, *The Book of the Dead*, by EA Wallis Budge, published by Arkana, Penguin, and RO Faulkner's translations, *The Ancient Egyptian Pyramid Texts* and *The Ancient Egyptian Coffin Texts* (in three volumes), both published by Aris and Phillips, and strongly recommend that the reader refer to these original sources for a deeper understanding of Egyptian religious thought.

As with Egyptian art, when one first looks at Egyptian literature, it is completely baffling, as one enters an almost surreal world of bizarre concepts and happenings. The most striking impression one has of reading the texts just mentioned is the kaleidoscopic, phantasmagoric atmosphere of much of what is described: as in a hallucinogenic dreamscape, everything keeps shifting and changing, as one thing becomes another, a deity is part of another deity, an entity has many names and many forms, and the speaker himself, the magician, becomes them all. This is the domain of the shaman or priest-magus as he wrestles to command both the powers of nature and the forces in his own unconscious mind: it can by turns be an ecstatically blissful experience or one of nightmarish horror. At one moment, the magician is a very god, triumphant and all-powerful; the next, he is in danger of going upside down through the underworld and eating filth, as the forces of chaos and the terrors in his own unconscious mind threaten to overwhelm him. Yet throughout the ordeal he must prevail, by his invocation of the gods, by knowing the right words to use, the right names and the right way to utter them, and above all by his own spiritual purity.

In the oldest texts it is the king alone who has these magical techniques: it is he who mounts boldly to the sky, enters the heavenly realms and demands, with threats if need be, that the deities recognize him as one of them, a divine being; for he has come to claim by right his iron throne among the stars. Well he might, for the king was perceived as a god on earth – as the sun god Horus himself. In the so-called Cannibal Hymn (*Pyramid Texts*, Utterances 273–4), he is even eating the gods, claiming their power as his own by actually consuming their very being – big ones for breakfast, medium-sized ones for lunch, and little ones for supper!

By the time that the *Book of the Dead* was compiled, other people – nobles, officials, scribes and others who could afford the requisite funerary preparations – also sought entry into the hallowed spheres of the afterlife. They too wished to be transformed upon death into shining spirits and imperishable stars, and sought to enter the Halls of Osiris to have their hearts weighed in the balance of Maat, to be judged worthy and admitted to eternal life. To do this, they needed to know all the correct passwords to get through the gates of the underworld and overcome all the demons en route, so that they might finally come into the divine presence of the Lord of Eternity, the Prince of Everlastingness – the risen Osiris who had himself triumphed over death and had the power to grant to his followers the ability to do likewise.

Although these texts were written to help the spirits of the dead in the afterlife, it is very doubtful that the skills they impute to the practitioner were believed to be acquired only in the postmortem mode of being. The pharaoh was not only a god but a powerful magician while on earth: indeed, he was the magician par excellence. In theory, all the religious rites performed in temples were performed solely by the king, though in practice, this was through the agency of his deputies, the priests. Indeed, it was the king who kept the very cosmos in operation by means of his magic. If every aspect of life for the ordinary Egyptian was religious and spiritual, for the king this was taken to extremes; his entire life was one long religious ritual. When he rose in the morning, took his ritual bath, dressed in his ceremonial robes and mounted the ceremonial staircase in the Temple of the Morning, he was not simply emulating the sun god bathing in the clouds of dawn and rising in the heavens: in a very real sense he was the sun god. If the pharaoh failed to perform these actions, then the sun itself would no doubt fail to rise: Apep, the dark serpent of chaos, would overwhelm the powers of light and truth. The divine order of the world, Maat – which, like all divine principles or *neteru*, could be personified as a deity, in this case a goddess, and is also the very foundation of the world, the *ben-ben* stone or primeval mound on which the god Atum-Ra raised himself up in the First Time to bring all Creation into being – would be utterly overwhelmed and engulfed in the waters of Nun, the primordial ocean. This must never be allowed to happen, and so everything in existence was totally dependent on the pharaoh and the correct performance of his magical-religious duties. Thus was magic at the very heart of the Egyptian state, and the pharaoh was the greatest magician of them all.

Those who claimed magical abilities in death must have been initiated into the mysteries during life. The king claimed his place in heaven by right, for he was born royal and ascended to the throne as a god; but there is good reason to suppose that even the king received intensive magical instruction, for in ancient Egypt it was absolutely unthinkable that anyone holding a position of public office should not be a skilled magician. Those other than the pharaoh who aspired to an immortal state after death had to earn that right through virtuous living and training in the magical arts. Magic in Egypt was not, as it became within Christian culture, the preserve of the solitary eccentric or anti-establishment rebel, but was institutionalized in the highest echelons of society.

When we read the *Pyramid Texts*, *Coffin Texts* and *Book of the Dead*, therefore, we should not think of the events described as being peculiar to the postmortem condition. The beliefs expressed in these texts were held throughout life, and apply as much in this world as in the next. Because of this, it is possible to use some of the material to compose seasonal rites, as in this book. We have attempted to present the material as far as possible just as it stands, without distorting it, altering it, or inserting any wording of our own invention. Apart from the words of the priest at the end of each rite, thanking the deities who have been invoked, all the speeches in these rites are faithful renderings of ancient Egyptian texts by respected translators. There are therefore no pseudo-archaisms or New Age ideas of the sort which so often appear in rites for modern Pagans. Everything, as far as possible, is authentic ancient Egyptian tradition.

At a first reading, it is inevitable that some of the concepts and imagery may be hard to understand. Partly this may be because of difficulties of translation: indeed, some ancient Egyptian terms are untranslatable. Some phrases are puzzling because they allude to symbolism and mythological situations which cannot be identified. We have made no attempt to amend awkward passages, which must speak for themselves, such as they can. To help the reader, in a short section at the start of each rite, we have explained some of the terms which appear in the rite that follows, and have also included a glossary at the back of the book. These sacred, mystical, magical, poetic texts are masterpieces of the world's religious literature, and if in places they have been rendered incomprehensible through their long journey down the ages and translation into the language of a foreign culture, then to a certain extent we have to bear with it. It seems like a miracle that we are able to read them at all: only many, many years of research and effort by egyptologists, translators and linguists has made this possible.

Egyptian Mythology, the Seasons and Environment

While not tampering with the texts themselves, one adaptation which we have been obliged to make is to compose the rites so that they are suitable for use by modern Pagans living in Britain. For this, they have to fit the seasons as we experience them here in Britain today. Most modern Pagans mark the seasonal changes by celebrating the Greater and Lesser Sabbats, or solstices, equinoxes, and the cross-quarter days called Celtic Fire Festivals. In total there are eight festivals, evenly distributed round the year.

It is important to recognize that the ancient Egyptians did not celebrate all these festivals, or in the cases where they had a festival at the same time of the year as we do, it did not necessarily have the same significance. The most radical difference is that the Egyptian harvest festival was in the spring, and the ploughing and seed-planting festival was in the autumn; summer was the dead time of year, and winter was the time of fertility. If we were to place the rites at the time of year when the Egyptians would have celebrated them, this would be the complete reverse of seasonal conditions over most of the world's northern hemisphere today. The reason for this is that there were unique circumstances in Egypt caused by the flooding of the Nile, which fertilized an otherwise barren land.

Egyptian Pagan mythology is intrinsically connected to the natural environment of Egypt. The country was called the Two Lands, which ostensibly referred to Upper Egypt and Lower Egypt; but it also referred to the Black Land of the Nile's flood plain and the Red Land of the desert. ('The Two Lands' may also have referred to heaven and earth, for the Egyptians thought of their country as being an image of the heavens, with the Nile corresponding to the Milky Way.) The Red Land, where humans could die of thirst and hunger under the relentlessly burning heat of the sun, was the domain of the red-haired Set, god of chaos and destruction. The Black Land was the domain of his gentle brother Osiris, who, in his name of Great Black, was the principle of dormant fertility in the cthonic realm, and, in his name of Great Green, was the principle of resurrection sprouting in the plant growth which turned the Black Land green after the retreat of the annual inundation. During the summer months, the heat of the blazing sun would shrivel all vegetation and parch the earth; for a while it would seem that the desert threatened to encroach on the habitable land, like red Set murdering his green brother Osiris. At the end of the summer, the Nile would flood – a momentous event which happened to correspond to the heliacal (dawn) rising of Sirius (or Sothis), the star of Isis, wife of Osiris – and so Isis found her dead husband in the black fertile soil emerging from the retreating flood-waters like the primordial mound or *ben-ben* on which the Creator stood at the dawn of the world. So was Maat, the divine principle of order, restored to the land after the devastation. The newly-planted seed began to sprout as Osiris when Isis restored him to life and conceived their son Horus – who was not only the sun god in heaven, but was incarnated on earth in the pharaoh, the legitimacy of whose reign was symbolized each time the desert retreated like the vanquished tyrant Set when Horus defeated him and assumed his rightful place on the throne.

The seasonal religious rites of the Egyptians, therefore, celebrate the actions of the gods – the *neteru* – both as they were in the First Time and as these actions are repeatedly made manifest in the workings of nature.

Ancient Egyptian Rites in a Modern Setting

One may raise the question of whether it makes sense to worship ancient foreign nature deities in the completely different context of modern urban Britain. We need to recognize that this is not just a recent decadent development: the *neteru* first came to Britain in the cult of Isis, brought here by the Romans nearly 2000 years ago. Isianism at that time had spread throughout the Roman Empire, promising salvation and eternal life to all the goddess's devotees under whatever name they knew her. Outside her native land, Isis flourished, becoming, in the words of the second-century writer Apuleius, *deorum dearumque facies uniformis* – all gods and all goddesses in a single form – and she was given the title *myrionymos,* 'having ten thousand names', because she was thought to be all deities of all cultures and all pantheons, under their various different names. She thus became the Supreme Being, and her cult was such a serious rival to that of Christianity that it was never completely destroyed, even when Paganism was suppressed by law, but rather it became incorporated as the cult of the Virgin Mary.

Archeological finds in London, York and Silchester indicate that Isis had her temples there. It used to be thought that the Romans during their occupation remained segregated from the indigenous population of Britain; but more recent research suggests that this was not the case. Roman culture permeated out from the military centres into the population as a whole, carrying with it religious and spiritual ideas which became syncretized with native beliefs. We can assume, therefore, that Isianism would have found some converts among the Britons. When the Roman army left Britain, after more than 300 years, many Romans, including, it may be assumed, some Isiacs, stayed behind, integrating into the already Romanized British culture.

Isianism was very much an urban form of the religion: the goddess's temples tended to be in city centres, often near to the market place, where they were readily accessible to the ordinary people. From having originally been the patroness of pharaonic power – her very name in Egyptian, Aset, meaning 'throne' – Isis adapted with apparent ease to become the champion of the poor, the suffering and the sick, who could identify with the goddess's earthly trials, and hope, with her help, to overcome adversity as she had done.

There is an important sense in which Egyptian Paganism is not a foreign religion at all. Just as much as it makes reference to the Egyptian landscape, it makes reference to the sun and the stars. The sun is the same sun everywhere on the planet, and the stars which the ancient Egyptians saw can be seen today from Britain. As we gaze up at the winter sky, we too can see the celestial form of Osiris, shining as the constellation of Orion, 'one who strides far to the limit of [his] desire'; and we too can see Isis, just as the Egyptians saw her, as Sirius, close behind him – the brightest star in the heavens. On a summer's day we, like the ancient Egyptians, can see also the goddess of love and beauty, Hathor, as the sun, 'the mistress of splendour on the paths of the cloudy sky'. As long as the ancient texts can come alive for us in this way, Egyptian Paganism cannot be alien to us.

Even in its original setting, it had a quality which makes it suitable to adapt to an urban context. As already explained, we tend to associate Paganism with rustic peasant traditions, largely due to a misconception. Allied to this is the notion that Paganism is about the wildness of nature in all its raw power, but this is not true of all forms of Paganism. For the ancient Egyptians, wilderness did not have the romantic appeal that it may have for us: wilderness, to the Egyptian mind, was the harsh, dangerous desert, the Red Land of Set, which threatened to destroy the order of the world and pitch it into chaos. The Black Land of Osiris, on the other hand, was a very orderly place, given over to agriculture in a neatly-arranged patchwork of fields interspersed with cottages and hamlets. Religious rites

conducted by the priesthood did not take place in a natural environment, but in the artificially illuminated gloom of massive stone
temples. It is therefore entirely appropriate to perform Egyptian rites
indoors.

It is true, however, that chaotic or uncontrolled elements were
sometimes permitted to impinge on the religious festivities, as in the
intoxicated celebrations at the festival of Hathor, in which the
common people participated. Ordinary people, of course, would have
had folk forms of the religion which may have been quite different
from that practised by an educated priesthood in the temples. In a
significant way, the Egyptian lifestyle was also dependent on the completely uncontrolled intervention of chaos in the annual inundation,
which was not always a benign event, for property might be
destroyed by a high flood, and casualties and fatalities could not
always be avoided. The floodwater would even enter some of the
temples! To drown in the Nile might be considered a particularly
blessed form of death, as one was taken by the god, but it was scarcely
something to be celebrated. It was the resultant fertility of the land
and the restoration of Maat after the water subsided which was the
real cause for celebration, and not the unpredictable, unpleasant
side-effects. Overall, the ancient Egyptians sought orderliness, justice,
balance and control, and these were only to be found in a thoroughly
domesticated, civilized environment – not in the uncouth wilds.

This, then, is a form of Paganism very suited to the modern way
of life. If there are aspects of Egyptian religion which are incomprehensible to us now, other aspects resonate with modern concerns and
modes of thought. For all its emphasis on balance, order and justice,

Egyptian Paganism is by no means a sanitized religion. There are areas of Egyptian religious thought which have been described as 'primitive', but these stand alongside more sophisticated developments. We must not forget that Egypt is in Africa, and some aspects of Egyptian religion are similar to religious beliefs from other parts of Africa: as a magical religion, for instance, it has something in common with Voodoo (which is based on African beliefs).

The Egyptians were religiously conservative, preserving rituals, prayers, deities and customs which to a certain way of thinking may seem to have long outgrown their usefulness; but nothing was discarded, nothing rejected. This lends a curious atmosphere to many of the religious texts, in which a raw primitivism seems to lurk beneath a sophisticated veneer. Just as the sun god must fight off the chaos serpent at the beginning and ending of each day, so it seems that the Egyptian was aware of an ongoing battle in the psyche between the light of reason and the dark chaos of forces in the unconscious. After life's day came the dark night of death, the fading of consciousness, and the confrontation with those very powers. The unwary, untrained traveller in the underworld could experience total psychological collapse and disintegration: only the accomplished magician could triumph through force of will and moral purity of the spirit, maintaining his psychic integrity by means of his moral integrity. In a post-Freudian age, we may find new meaning in such concepts, and what may once have seemed like crude superstition could be interpreted in another way as a sensitive awareness of human psychology.

The Neteru: Egyptian Deities

The Egyptian word *neter* (plural *neteru*) is translated as 'god', but this is not a particularly accurate translation: 'divine principle' might be better. If we try to understand Egyptian *neteru* in terms of concepts derived from, say, a Greek view of the gods, then we shall very quickly become confused. When Pagan deities are mentioned, very often people ask, 'And what is that the god of?' It is common to think of Pagan deities along the lines of the god of wisdom, the goddess of love, and so on; but this approach to the Egyptian *neteru* is likely to raise as many questions as it answers.

For a start, the Egyptians had literally hundreds of *neteru*, and they cannot be conveniently categorized in terms of their functions or areas of expertise. While some of the *neteru* resemble Greek deities, in that they are anthropomorphic beings with distinct personalities, others are more like personifications – abstract concepts described in anthropomorphic terms. The goddess Isis is an example of the former, whereas

Maat, Heka and Sia are more like the latter. Some *neteru* are best described as indwelling spirits in material phenomena: for example, Nut (pronounced 'Noot'), the sky, and Geb (pronounced 'Geeb' with a hard G), the earth, are conceived of as divine beings.

This approach reveals that Egyptian Paganism was originally an animistic religion: spirit was seen to be everywhere – even in what we would think of as inanimate objects – and the entire cosmos was numinous with the divine. This also explains why some *neteru* have animal forms, for if Deity was everywhere and in everything, then an animal could be a manifestation of a god. Some *neteru* had their own sacred animals which were kept in temples and treated like the gods themselves: for example, the Apis Bull, which was a manifestation of Ptah, lived like a god-king, the pharaoh himself, and would be afforded a royal funeral and burial when he died.

It is a strange characteristic of the *neteru*, which is at first extremely confusing, that one *neter* may become another *neter*, be part of another *neter*'s body, or be the same *neter* under a different name. For example, the Eye of Ra, the sun god, is that god's eye, the serpent (uraeus) on his brow, and the physical sun itself. It is also a separate goddess, Hathor. Sometimes, however, Hathor, the gentle cow, becomes Sekhmet, the raging lioness. The goddess Bast, or Bastet, the cat, may also be seen as a docile form of Sekhmet, and therefore analogous to Hathor. Quite often, Hathor is assimilated to Isis, and these two goddesses are represented with almost identical appearance and insignia. In one sense it would be completely wrong to say that all these goddesses are the same goddess, but in another sense, which is explained below, it would be quite true to say that all deities are one and the same, for they all emanate from the same Divine Source.

A similar confusion may arise with regard to the male gods. In Heliopolis, the Creator was called Ra; in Hermopolis, he was Thoth; in Memphis, he was Ptah; in Thebes, he was Amun; and he was also known as Atum. It would be quite wrong to regard all these *neteru* as one and the same *neter*, for each has his individual myth and iconography. Yet, there is a sense in which the Creation stories may be taken as variations of the same story, compatible with one another in many respects, if one takes a poetical, metaphorical approach to understanding them. Ra is the Creator as the sun, the physical source of life, who creates the world by generating it from his own substance. Thoth, or Tehuti, is the Divine Mind, who creates intellectually, uttering a Word of Power. Ptah is the craftsman, the architect of the universe, the sculptor who moulds human beings, rather like Khnum, another Creator deity, who forms them on his potter's wheel. The name Amun means 'hidden'; Atum means 'whole', 'entirety' and 'complete'. If we believe in a Creator deity, then surely all these ideas of such a Being must apply. The Egyptians did not see these concepts as mutually exclusive, for each view contributes to a more complete picture and a better understanding of Deity. In difficult areas of theology, where we confront the profound and ineffable, there is room for more than one dogmatic 'truth'; for understanding in religious terms is more of an art than a science. The ancient Egyptians recognized this and therefore were much more happy to accept what, to our modern, scientifically-oriented minds, often seem like contradictions and incoherent notions.

Now, to return to the point raised earlier, about the sense in which all the *neteru* may be regarded as manifestations of a single deity, we shall explain the concept of the *ennead*. In Egyptian theology, an *ennead* is a group of nine *neteru*, though in some instances the group may contain more than nine. The term is usually translated as 'company of the gods'. In the various cult centres, depending on the major deity who was venerated there, the deities comprising the *ennead* could vary. (Sometimes there was a secondary *ennead*, in which case the groups would be termed 'greater' and 'lesser'.) The nine deities plus the main god therefore made up a group of ten, and it is possible to regard these ten deities as aspects of one deity.

For those familiar with the Cabala, the Jewish system of mysticism, the idea of the *ennead* is interesting: for in Cabala too, there is the theory that Creation was formed through ten emanations (called *Sephiroth*) from an ineffable Source, the lowest being the material world and the highest being the most sublime concept of godhead, *Kether*, the Crown. The Hebrews lived for generations in Egypt, and Moses was brought up as an Egyptian prince; and it seems likely that the Cabala developed in the Hellenistic culture of Alexandria in the early centuries AD, where Egyptian, Greek and Jewish theological and philosophical ideas were widely discussed among the intellectual populace. It therefore seems possible, or even likely, that there is a direct connection here between Egyptian and Jewish theologies.

In Heliopolis, where the 'official' form of Egyptian religion (that most closely associated with the pharaonic cult) was practised, the chief deity was Ra–Atum, as already mentioned, and the other members of the *ennead* were as follows: Shu, the god of the atmosphere;

Tefnut, the goddess of moisture, wife of Shu; Nut, the goddess of the sky; Geb, the god of the earth, husband of Nut; Osiris, god of plant growth, death and resurrection; Set, god of chaos and passion; Isis, goddess of magic, wife of Osiris; and Nephthys, twin sister of Isis and wife of Set. (Though we have briefly described them with these attributes, to provide a general picture, as already explained, with Egyptian deities this can be misleading, so should not be applied too rigidly.) Horus, not a member of the standard *ennead*, could be included as the fifth child of Nut and Geb. These nine *neteru* comprise three divine generations, for Shu and Tefnut, the offspring of Ra, are the parents of Nut and Geb, who are the parents of the other five *neteru*. These nine *neteru*, therefore, are the children, grandchildren and great-grandchildren of the supreme deity, Ra-Atum; but they may also be conceived of as emanations of one divine, ineffable Being who, according to the Heliopolitan Creation myth, came into being as the one who 'comes into being, coming into being as all the things which came into being'. In the ancient Egyptian language, his evolutions are described thus: *Nuk pu kheper em Khepera. Kheper-na kheper kheperu; kheper kheperu neb ... Kheper asht kheperu nu kheperu em kheperu nu mesu, em kheperu nu mesu sen.* (EA Wallis Budge, *The Gods of the Egyptians*, Dover, 1969.)

This description of the Creation, which sounds like a magical incantation, is based on a pun on the divine name of Khepera ('the one who comes into being'), the scarab beetle who is a form of the sun god Ra as Creator. In Egyptian thought, it was entirely acceptable, without contradiction, that the sun could be a ball rolled across the sky by the beetle god Khepera, the golden falcon Horus, the Eye of Ra, the serpent of power on the brow of the Supreme Being, a boat (the solar bark), the docile cow goddess Hathor, the fierce lioness Sekhmet, the softly sensuous cat goddess Bast, and Ra himself. Ra, as Khepera, comes into being not only as the sun, but as all life generated by the sun, the offspring of his children, grand-children and great-grandchildren, while human beings are the tears shed from his eye – another pun, based on the similarity of the ancient Egyptian words for 'tears' and 'humans' (the Egyptians were fond of puns).

An *ennead* was not venerated at all cult centres: at Hermopolis, there was an *ogdoad*, which was a similar concept to the *ennead*, being a group of eight (rather than nine) deities.

Nowadays, people tend to think of God as a remote Being – so remote, in fact, that his existence is even in doubt. To the modern mind, the world appears to be a spiritually dead place, with human beings the only intelligent form of life. To the ancient Egyptians, on the other hand, Deity was close and intimate, manifesting in a myriad forms and in all aspects of human experience. The domestic cat was a manifestation of Bast, goddess of joy and fertility; the wild dog, or jackal, was a manifestation of Anubis, the guide of souls, helper of the dead; the ram was a manifestation of Amun; the cow was Hathor, goddess of love; the bull was Osiris; the lion was Sekhmet. The *neteru* were also present in situations and human emotions: so making love was a manifestation of Hathor, and fighting was a manifestation of Set. Under these influences, humans as well as animals became literally possessed by the gods, so there was no question of doubting their existence.

This direct experience of the gods is absolutely crucial to Egyptian Paganism. Central to the practice of the religion, and the magic which is inseparable from it, is the technique known to occultists as Assumption of the Godform. A more modern, popular term for this is 'channelling'. In the Bible, a similar technique is called 'prophesying', meaning not just telling the future, but being the mouthpiece of God, allowing Deity to speak directly through the human agent. To assume the godform, one speaks and acts as the deity or *neter* for the duration of the rite or for the relevant part of the rite. To do this, it is helpful to visualize the *neter* as clearly as possible and to see, in one's mind's eye, the form of this deity merging with one's own body. It is customary to imagine the *neter* entering from behind, the focus for the entry being the nape of the neck. Modern Pagans often stand with their backs to the altar to allow this process to take place at the start of the rite. At the end, they face the altar and visualize the deity leaving by the solar plexus – a region of the midriff which is supposed to be a point of psychic energy.

The Egyptian priests actually 'saw' the wall paintings of the deities in their temples come to life through invocations, step down from the walls and enter their own bodies when they assumed the god-form. (An image could therefore be very dangerous; so to protect against the hieroglyphic forms of snakes, lions and other harmful animals, these would be painted in two sections with a division through the middle, or with a knife through them, to render them harmless.) To help them to assume the forms of the deities, members of the Egyptian priesthood would dress up as the deities. The priest of Anubis would wear a dog's-head mask during the rites of embalming bodies, in which he played a key role, and it is likely that the priests and priestesses of other *neteru* would also have worn masks of their deities' totem animals. This may be why some deities are represented with animal heads on human bodies, for this was how they manifested through their masked priests. At the rites concerning the death and resurrection of Osiris, two priestesses, ritually purified by having their body hair removed, wearing woollen headbands, and each with the name of Isis or Nephthys written on her arm to identify her magically with the goddess she was representing, would sing hymns of mourning as the goddesses themselves. In this way, members of the priesthood actually became the deities whom they served, and this identification with the Divine was far deeper than merely symbolic.

In Christianity today, with its emphasis on sin and humility, it seems to be all too often forgotten that Jesus himself taught that the kingdom of heaven is within each person. Turning to Paganism, some people have tried to recover this sense of potential divinity within each of us, recognizing the mystical, alchemical undertaking of transmuting lead into gold, the human into the divine. This is nowhere more evident than in Egyptian Paganism (for Egypt, the land of Khem, was the place where alchemy originated and after which it is named). The Egyptians truly aspired to become *neteru* in the afterlife, and it is no mere idle boasting (as some egyptologists have unfortunately construed) when the deceased in the funerary texts speak of being the gods themselves. What we call the *Book of the Dead* was originally called the *Chapters of Coming Forth by Day*, this title referring to the divine magical power of shapeshifting, by which a spirit might manifest as, for example, a bird or animal. The justified dead, who were skilled magicians, attained this god-like power to change their shape and return to earth – not as reincarnations, but as spirit beings in animal form.

This was not just an idle hope for the afterlife, however; a sympathetic interpretation of ancient Egyptian beliefs as compared to those of shamanistic religions strongly suggests that accomplished magicians possessed the ability to shapeshift, explore the *Neterkhert*, encounter the gods, and indeed become the gods, while still alive, by using techniques for entering altered states of consciousness. Modern Pagans can learn to do this too, for the rites in this book are composed from actual texts which the Egyptians themselves would have used for precisely this purpose.

Concepts of
Egyptian Spirituality

There are certain terms and concepts employed by the ancient Egyptians which cannot be accurately translated because there is no modern English equivalent. Some attempts to translate them have actually obscured the true meaning by imposing a different idea altogether. The Egyptian words usually translated as 'underworld', 'soul' and 'spirit' are particularly problematical, and different commentators have provided different explanations.

The Egyptian words *Amentet* (or *Amenti*), *Neterkhert*, and *Tuat* are often translated as 'underworld', though this is highly misleading. *Amentet*, meaning 'the hidden place', is the realm of the dead, presided over by Osiris, and though it is sometimes identified with the underground regions through which the sun passes at night, it may also be simply 'the West' or the place of the setting sun. It was identified with the goddess of love, Hathor, and far from being a place of darkness, was considered to be of great beauty.

Osiris's realm was also thought to be in the night sky (and as such was identified with Nut), for the constellation of Orion was the soul of Osiris, and Sirius was his wife Isis, faithfully following behind. It was hoped that the deceased might become an *akh*, a shining spirit, or literally, a star in the constellation of Orion or among the circumpolar stars which never set and were therefore 'imperishable stars'. The afterlife, even when imagined as being under the earth, was by no means a shadowy or dark experience, and it could very well be a shining realm, quite literally in heaven.

The *Tuat* seems to be a region of the sky near to the horizon, associated with the morning twilight. However, there are various opinions about precisely what this term means. It may be regarded as the part of the sky where the gods are 'born' – that is, the eastern horizon where the sun and stars rise. This, though, may be only an entrance to the *Tuat*, along with the western horizon. The *Tuat* itself may be conceived of as an inner realm, inside the body of the night sky personified as the goddess Nut, who gives birth to the sun each morning and swallows him each night. It is like the womb of the goddess, filled with the divine, creative potential of things not yet made manifest.

The *Neterkhert*, meaning 'the divine under place', is another inner spiritual realm, but its location as 'under' something is not clear: perhaps it is not so much a place as a perception or way of seeing the world, as the shaman sees beneath the surface appearance of things to the spiritual, psychic realm which lies behind all material phenomena – the realm of spirits and the *neteru*, and the interconnecting web of magical forces and energies which give rise to all that happens.

In any case it is clear that the Greek notion of a murky under-world and Christian ideas of an underworld Hell as a place of torture do not apply to the Egyptian concepts signified by the words trans-lated as 'underworld'. Although Christians derived some ideas about Hell from depictions of the punishment of the followers of Apep, the chaos demons, this is largely due to a misunderstanding; for the souls of the dead were not thought to suffer such a fate in the Egyptian scheme of things.

The human being is spiritually and psychically complex in the Egyptian view. The terms *khat, khaibit, ka, ba, ab, akh* and *sahu*, identi-fying aspects of a soul and body, cause many problems for accurate translation. Though most of these need not concern us for the pur-pose of performing the rites in this book, for a proper understanding of Egyptian religious thought it is important to have some grasp of their meaning.

The *khat* is the physical body, but is really a term used only of a corpse.

The *khaibit* is a person's shadow, or ghost: it is a vehicle for nega-tive aspects of the personality, the lower nature, and was thought to linger around the tomb after death.

The *ka*, or 'double' as it tends to be translated, is a sort of spirit guide, or possibly an equivalent to the esoteric concept of the Higher Self, which, in the case of the common people, was closely associated with the spirits of the ancestors, although the pharaoh had his own individual *ka*. The *ka* is also spoken of as a general spiritual energy which may be possessed by an individual, a group of people, or a *neter*.

The *ba* is what we might call the astral body – the body in which the soul moves after death or during an out-of-body experience. Because an out-of-body experience is often one of floating or flying, the *ba* is conceptualized in the form of a bird with a human head.

The *ab* is the heart or essential essence of a person. It is not exactly the equivalent of the soul, since when it was weighed in the scales of the goddess Maat after death, it might testify against its owner, so it is more akin to the modern concept of the conscience.

The *akh*, as already mentioned, is a shining spirit: it is, however, the perfected *ba*, after all worldly desires and failings have been shed. It was thought that the *akh* would germinate out of the *ba*, like a plant growing from seed. 'Osiris beds' – planted seed-trays in the shape of Osiris – were placed in tombs to represent this spiritual resurrection.

The *sahu* or *sah* is the divine body which the *akh* occupies when it has attained the purely spiritual, perfected state in the realm of the afterlife.

The concept of the *ren*, the name of a person, was also extremely important, for the nameless person could not exist in the afterlife. Those guilty of particularly execrable crimes had their names removed or altered to become curses ('the god hates him'), or excised from monuments in the case of kings and officials. Without a name, the person's spirit was consigned to oblivion.

It is clear from all this that the ancient Egyptians had a very complex, sophisticated understanding of the psychic and spiritual realms and of the postmortem condition. One has the strong impression, however, that this view was not 'otherworldly' in any real sense, for the otherworld interacted with this world in so many ways. The spirits of the dead were not remote, any more than the gods were remote, for, like the *neteru*, they could 'come forth by day' in myriad shapes and forms and were never far away from their living descendants who tended the tomb, made regular food offerings and kept alive the *ren* or name of the deceased person.

Morality and correct living were also of the highest importance to the ancient Egyptians. There is a modern conceit that ancient Paganism was a morally lax religion, and modern Pagans still suffer prejudice from people who believe this about Paganism. The ancient Egyptians were in no doubt that the way in which one lived in this life would determine the conditions in which one lived in the next. Only the morally upright person could hope to enjoy an afterlife with the gods in the Field of Rushes – that most pleasant part of the heavenly realm. There, the blessed dead were reunited with their deceased relatives (funerary papyri depict these happy scenes!) and enjoyed an idyllic rural existence in which all the hard work was done by *shabtis* – spirit androids provided in the afterlife by virtue of little statuettes of slaves placed for this purpose in tombs.

For the morally lax person, the postmortem experience was likely to be very different. If he lied to the Forty-Two Assessors in the Hall of the Double Maati and his heart testified against him, weighing down the scales of Maat when put in the balance against the goddess's feather of truth, then a fearful monster called Ammut, having the body of a hippopotamus and the jaws of a crocodile, would devour the heart, and therefore the soul, of the miscreant. It is possible, however, that all was not lost, for this goddess may be a form of the hippopotamus goddess Tauret, who was the patroness of childbirth: in which case, the soul that suffered this fate may simply have been destined to reincarnate.

To qualify as one of the justified dead, one had to make the so-called Negative Confession in the presence of Osiris's Forty-Two Assessors, denying that one was guilty of a range of crimes and misdemeanours, including murder, blasphemy, desecration of a temple, contamination of a water supply, adultery, causing someone to weep, and eating one's heart out (envy).

It is plain that the ancient Egyptians had very stringent moral standards. Egyptian books of proverbs and advice about how to live wisely advocate a quiet, moderate way of life. The prudent person is to avoid heavy drinking, brawling and engaging in conflict, and is instead to behave courteously and considerately towards others, especially the frail, poor and elderly, and always to honour the gods. Only a person of integrity can hope for a blessed afterlife in the company of the *neteru*.

Finally in this chapter, we shall mention another concept which was very important to the ancient Egyptians – the *Zep Tepi*, the First Time or Primeval Time. If we were to think of this simply as a time long, long ago, again we should be distorting a concept which had quite a different significance to the ancient Egyptians. The *Zep Tepi* was certainly a time long ago, a Golden Age when the *neteru* were living on earth and Maat prevailed everywhere; but the *Zep Tepi* is also mythological time, and therefore can be seen as almost a separate dimension in which the exploits of the gods take place and which may be accessible to people at any time. Being able to evoke, as it were, a *Zep Tepi* event, was essential for the working of magic.

A typical example of this is the Legend of Ra and Isis, which was originally a spell to cure a snake bite. In the story, Isis, plotting to obtain magical powers from Ra, makes a snake from mud mixed with Ra's saliva. The snake bites Ra, who is obliged to reveal to Isis his secret name, the source of all his power, so that she may use it to banish the poison from his body. The magician–healer would identify with Isis while telling this story to the patient, who would identify with Ra. At the end, the magician would assume the godform of Isis and command the poison to leave the patient's body: because in the story Ra had been healed, so would the patient be healed, according to the theory of sympathetic magic. By assuming the godform, the magician would actually be channelling the power of Isis through to the patient to effect a cure. The *Zep Tepi* event thus became potent in the present. Healing spells often took this form, with Isis as the healer and Horus or Ra as the patient. A similar spell could be used for malign purposes. An enemy could be identified with the Apep serpent which is defeated by Ra: as Ra triumphs over Apep each day, so will the magician triumph over his enemy.

The *Zep Tepi* was therefore a constantly accessible divine realm where the acts of the gods could become operative in the here and now. Though it was the Golden Age long ago, between the time when the Creator rose on the primeval mound at the first dawn and the time when Set murdered his brother, the good king Osiris, the *Zep Tepi* could return at any time. Horus, Osiris's rightful heir, re-established the First Time when he defeated his wicked uncle Set and ascended to the throne of his father. So did each pharaoh, the incarnation of Horus, make things as they were in the First Time, and commemorative stelae attest to this fact. Nowadays we value the pioneering and innovative; but the pharaohs of ancient Egypt would achieve all that could possibly be desired by making things as they were in the First Time, for no condition could be more perfect.

In their book *Keeper of Genesis*, Robert Bauval and Graham Hancock have put forward the haunting idea that the *Zep Tepi*, when Osiris reigned on earth, was in the Age of Leo, when the constellation of Orion (Osiris) was at his lowest point in the sky: this was the First Time of Osiris. Over the centuries, the stars gradually change their position in the sky in relation to the earth, because of the slight 'wobble' as the earth turns on its axis; so Orion is now, at the dawning of the Age of Aquarius, at his highest point in the sky. According to this view, we are now living in the Last Time of Osiris – a time, perhaps of apocalyptic happenings, or even a Second Coming!

Nevertheless, Second Coming or not, we who live in the Last Time will find that Osiris and the other *neteru* are alive for us today if we employ the methods of the ancient magicians. The Egyptian texts still speak to us, and by performing the rites contained in the following pages, perhaps we too may experience things as they were in the First Time, in the *Zep Tepi*.

About the Rites

Each of the eight rites presented here is designed for a small group working in a domestic environment. The rites therefore do not require a great deal of space or any special equipment which is not readily available. Each rite is designed for four people: ideally, a priest and priestess, another man, and another woman. (The part of the First Participant is written for a man, and that of the Second Participant for a woman, but in some of the rites, this gender distinction is not important.) With a few changes, they could be adapted for two or three people.

In each rite, a god and goddess are invoked, in some cases the emphasis being on the male, and in some cases on the female. The Priest and Priestess roles are intended for those participants who wish to assume the godforms of those deities being invoked. In some rites, the other participants also have an opportunity to assume godforms.

The ancient Egyptians would not have performed their rites inside a magic circle, but modern Pagans who are used to working in a circle may feel uneasy about working without. A circle may be cast formally by drawing a line around the working area with a wand, and visualizing the line as a barrier of light to keep out unwanted psychic influences. This line is actually the circumference of a complete sphere enclosing the participants and all their ritual equipment, and should be visualized as such.

Pagans who are accustomed to working within a consecrated circle may cast the circle in the usual way, but instead of summoning the traditional Elemental Kings to guard the quarters, it is advisable to call on the Four Sons of Horus, who are the Egyptian equivalent. There is no consensus as to which of these deities corresponds to which element, or to which quarter each should be assigned, but we have found the following arrangement to be successful: Qebhsennuf (pronounced 'Kebsnoof'), the falcon, in the east, representing air; Duamutef, the jackal, in the south, representing fire; Imsety, the man, in the west, representing water; and Hapi (pronounced 'Haahpi'), the baboon or dog-faced ape, in the north, representing earth. They should be visualized with human mummiform bodies and the heads of the relevant creatures. (Sometimes, Duamutef and Imsety were regarded as female.) They should not be summoned and banished in the masterful way that one usually addresses elementals, because the Sons of Horus are demigods and deserve more respect; if you ask them politely to come and guard the circle and witness the rites, and then thank them and say goodbye at the end, they will behave in a dignified way and will not play pranks, as some elementals are reputed to do. The Egyptian priesthood did not cast a circle for religious rites, but they were working inside consecrated temples; so you should do whatever you feel is appropriate in your circumstances.

All the rites here open with the same two prayers – one for lighting the candles and one for lighting the incense. The candle prayer, which is a spell from the *Book of the Dead* for kindling a torch in the underworld, identifies the flame with the shining Eye of Horus which banishes spiritual darkness as well as physical darkness. This is an act of psychic protection, ensuring that only benign entities will attend the proceedings. The two sisters of Ra, referred to in this prayer, are Isis and Nephthys, the sisters of Osiris, who is sometimes identified with Ra.

The censing prayer, which is spoken as the incense is lit, is the only text to which we have made significant alterations. The original form was written in the first person singular: 'Your perfume comes to me ... May my perfume come to you ...' and so on. This has been altered to take into account that four people are present, changing 'I' to 'we', 'me' to 'us' and 'my' to 'our', but is not indicated in the text itself by marking the substituted words with the customary square brackets, because ten pairs of square brackets in one prayer would be very distracting to the reader. For the original version of the prayer, please see Utterance 269 in *The Ancient Egyptian Pyramid Texts*, translation by RO Faulkner (Aris and Phillips). Alterations of this nature in other texts have been indicated with square brackets around the substituted wording, and in places where we have omitted words, this is indicated with ellipses (...). The words in italics between speeches are instructions, not to be spoken.

A sistrum decorated with the face of Hathor

In each rite, a place is allowed for meditation after the invocations are complete. The participants should sit quietly, with eyes closed, and try to allow their minds to be free of mundane thoughts. Ideas and images stimulated by the invocations should then begin to arise in the tranquil mind. It is at this point that the *neteru* themselves may communicate, appearing as a vision in the mind's eye or speaking to the mind's ear. If you have never tried this before, do not be discouraged if nothing very striking happens on the first few occasions. At first, one may experience only fleeting impressions, but with practice this will improve. One may be inclined to think, is this not just imagination? Yes, it is imagination, but the magician knows that imagination is a very powerful faculty. In an altered state of consciousness induced by ritual, the unconscious mind becomes accessible, intuition and even psychic faculties may be awakened, and the gods themselves may communicate by means of symbols in the unconscious. Some people think that the *neteru* are no more than the archetypes of the collective unconscious. Certainly they manifest by means of the archetypes, but it may well be that there really is a Divine Being behind these manifestations, so any messages or visions received should not be dismissed as mere idle daydreams.

When performing the rites, it is helpful to have a sistrum (plural, sistra). This is an ancient musical instrument sacred to the goddesses Hathor and Isis, and consists of a number of metal discs strung on wires across a frame supported on a long handle. When it is shaken, it makes a jangling, tinkling or clattering noise which was thought to banish evil spirits and honour the gods. Sistra are quite rare, but are obtainable from some occult outlets. A tambourine, maracas, a rattle, or even some small objects shaken inside a tin, would produce a similar sound, so you could use these instead if you do not have a sistrum.

Imbolc: 2 February

For modern Pagans, the Celtic Fire Festival of Imbolc is important as the first festival of the year, celebrating the return of the sun's light. The darkest part of the year's cycle has passed, and the first spring flowers are beginning to appear, so it is a time of hope for people living in cold, dark countries, very different from Egypt.

Since the ancient Egyptians had a festival of Nut on the first and second days of February, celebrating her birthday, and they also had (in the *Book of the Dead*) a spell to be recited in honour of the sun god on the last day of the second month of winter, we have included both this spell and two hymns to Nut in this rite.

A few words and names which appear here need to be explained. Heru-khuti is the god of the rising sun, a form of Horus. Tem or Temu is the god of the setting sun. A *khu* is a spirit. Het-benbenet is the House of the Pyramidion or *ben-ben* stone, the dwelling place of the sun god. The Tuat (pronounced 'Dwat') is the part of the sky where the sun rises. The season of pert is winter. The Utchat is the Eye of Horus, the moon, which was damaged by Set and restored by Thoth. 'Tamt' is a name signifying the universal god. 'Sekhem', meaning 'power', is a title of Ra and some other gods. 'The children of impotent rebellion' mentioned at the end of the rite are the followers of Apep and Set, and are the forces opposed to Ra's Creation – chaotic powers which he defeats every day.

The litany presented here is an extract from the beginning of a very long prayer called the Seventy-Five Praises of Ra, which identifies many deities with Ra. It is apparent from this that in Egyptian theology, as in all sophisticated forms of Paganism and as believed by most modern Pagans, the various gods and goddesses are aspects of one Supreme Being who is beyond human comprehension but who is recognized in various forms and manifestations.

IMBOLC RITE

The Triumph of Ra
and the Blessing of Nut

Cast the circle in the usual way and, if desired, call on Qebhsennuf in the East, Duamutef in the South, Imsety in the West and Hapi in the North for protection.

Two candles on the altar are unlit at start of rite. Incense is also unlit. The Priestess has a sistrum.

Shake sistrum.

Light the candles.

FIRST PARTICIPANT: The shining Eye of Horus cometh. The brilliant Eye of Horus cometh. It cometh in peace, it sendeth forth rays of light unto Ra in the horizon, and it destroyeth the powers of Set, according to the decree. It leadeth them on and it taketh possession of him, and its flame is kindled against him. Its flame cometh and goeth about, and bringeth adoration; it cometh and goeth about

heaven in the train of Ra upon the two hands of thy two sisters, O Ra. The Eye of Horus liveth, yea liveth.

Light the incense.

SECOND PARTICIPANT:

The fire is laid, the fire shines;

The incense is laid on the fire, the incense shines.

Your perfume comes to us, O Incense;

May our perfume come to you, O Incense:

Your perfume comes to us, you gods;

May our perfume come to you, you gods;

May we be with you, you gods;

May you be with us, you gods.

May we live with you, you gods;

May you live with us, you gods.

We love you, you gods;

May you love us, you gods.

Shake sistrum.

PRIEST: The divine Power hath risen and shineth in the horizon, and the god Tem hath risen out of the odour of that which floweth from him. The Khus shine in heaven and Het-benbenet rejoiceth, for there is among them a form which is like unto themselves; and there are shouts and cries of gladness within the shrine, and the sounds of those who rejoice go round about through the underworld, and homage is paid unto him at the decree of Tem and Heru-khuti.

PRIESTESS: His Majesty ordereth the company of the gods to follow in the train of his Majesty; his Majesty ordereth the calling of the Utchat ... His divine Eye resteth upon its seat with His Majesty at that hour of the night on the day of the fulfilment of the fourth hour of the beautiful land, on the last day of the second month of the season of pert. The Majesty of the Utchat is in the presence of the company of the gods, and his Majesty shineth as he shone in the primeval time, when the Utchat was first upon his head.

Shake sistrum.

PRIEST: Praise be to thee, O Ra, exalted Sekhem, lord of the hidden circles of the Tuat, bringer of forms, thou restest in secret places and makest thy creations in the form of the god Tamt.

PRIESTESS: Praise be to thee, O Ra, exalted Sekhem, thou creative force, who spreadest out thy wings, who restest in the Tuat, who makest the created things which come forth from his divine limbs.

FIRST PARTICIPANT: Praise be to thee, O Ra, exalted Sekhem, Ta-thenen, begetter of his gods. Thou art he who protecteth what is in him, and thou makest thy creations as Governor of thy Circle.

SECOND PARTICIPANT: Praise be to thee, O Ra, exalted Sekhem, looker on the earth, and brightener of Amenti. Thou art he whose forms are his own creations, and thou makest thy creations in thy Great Disk.

PRIEST: Praise be to thee, O Ra, exalted Sekhem, the Word-soul, that resteth on his high place. Thou art he who protecteth thy hidden spirits, and they have form in thee.

PRIESTESS: Praise be to thee, O Ra, exalted Sekhem, mighty one, bold of face, the knitter together of his body. Thou art he who gathereth together thy gods when thou goest into thy hidden Circle.

FIRST PARTICIPANT: Praise be to thee, O Ra, exalted Sekhem. Thou dost call to thine Eye, and dost speak to thy head, and dost give breath to the souls in their places, and they receive it and have their forms in him.

SECOND PARTICIPANT: Praise be to thee, O Ra, exalted Sekhem, destroyer of thine enemies; thou art he who doth decree destruction for the dead.

PRIEST: Praise be to thee, O Ra, exalted Sekhem, the sender forth of light into his Circle; thou art he who maketh the darkness to be in his Circle and thou coverest those who are therein.

PRIESTESS: Praise be to thee, O Ra, exalted Sekhem, the illuminer of bodies in the horizons; thou art he who entereth into his Circle.

FIRST PARTICIPANT: Praise be to thee, O Ra, exalted Sekhem, support of the Circles of Ament; thou art indeed the body of Temu.

SECOND PARTICIPANT: Praise be to thee, O Ra, exalted Sekhem, the hidden support of Anpu; thou art indeed the body of Khepera.

PRIEST: Praise be to thee, O Ra, exalted Sekhem, whose duration of life is greater than that of her whose forms are hidden; thou art indeed the bodies of Shu.

PRIESTESS: Praise be to thee, O Ra, exalted Sekhem, the guide of Ra to his members; thou art indeed the bodies of Tefnut.

FIRST PARTICIPANT: Praise be to thee, O Ra, exalted Sekhem; thou dost make to be abundant the things which are of Ra in their seasons, and thou art indeed Geb.

SECOND PARTICIPANT: Praise be to thee, O Ra, exalted Sekhem, the mighty one who doth keep count of the things which are in him; thou art indeed the bodies of Nut.

PRIEST: Praise be to thee, O Ra, exalted Sekhem, the lord who advancest; thou art indeed Isis.

PRIESTESS: Praise be to thee, O Ra, exalted Sekhem, whose head shineth more than the things which are in front of him; thou art indeed the bodies of Nephthys.

FIRST PARTICIPANT: Praise be to thee, O Ra, exalted Sekhem, united is he in members, One, who gathereth together all seed; thou art indeed the bodies of Horus.

SECOND PARTICIPANT: Praise be to thee, O Ra, exalted Sekhem, thou shining one who dost send forth light upon the waters of heaven; thou art indeed the bodies of Nu.

PRIEST: Ra, Tem, Utchatet, Shu, Geb, Osiris, Set, Horus, Menth, Bah, Ra-er-Neheh, Tehuti [who travels eternity], Nut, Isis, Nephthys, Hathor [the victorious], Mert, Maat [and] Anpu [of the land] are the soul and body of Ra.

Shake sistrum.

PRIESTESS:
O Nut, spread yourself over your son Osiris,
and hide him from Set. Protect him, O Nut!
Have you come to hide your son?

PRIEST AS GEB:
O Nut! You became a spirit,
you waxed mighty in the belly of your mother Tefnut
    before you were born.
How mighty is your heart!
You stirred in the belly of your mother in your name
    of Nut,

you are indeed a daughter more powerful than her
    mother ...
O Great One who has become the sky!
You have the mastery, you have filled every place with
    your beauty,
the whole earth lies beneath you, you have taken
    possession thereof,
you have enclosed the whole earth and everything therein
    within your arms ...
As Geb shall I impregnate you in your name of sky,
I shall join the whole earth to you in every place.
O high above the earth! You are supported upon your
    father Shu,
but you have power over him,
he so loved you that he placed himself – and all things
    beside – beneath you
so that you took up into you every god with his heavenly
    barque,
and as 'a thousand souls is she' did you teach them
that they should not leave you – as the stars.

PRIESTESS:
O my mother Nut
stretch your wings over me.
Let me become like the imperishable stars,
    like the indefatigable stars.

May Nut extend her arms over me
and her name of
> 'She who extends her arms'
> chases away the shadows
> and makes the light shine everywhere.

FIRST PARTICIPANT:

O Great Being who is in the world of
    the Dead,
At whose feet is Eternity,
In whose hand is the always,
Come to me.

SECOND PARTICIPANT:

O great divine beloved Soul,
    who is in the mysterious abyss,
Come to me.

> *Shake sistrum.*
> *Meditation.*
> *Shake sistrum.*

PRIESTESS: The computation of the Utchat hath been made in the presence of the divine lord of this earth; it is full to the uttermost, and it resteth. And these gods are rejoicing on this day, and they have their hands beneath them, and the festival of every god having been celebrated, they say:

PRIEST: Hail, praise be unto thee, O thou who art as Ra, rejoice in him, for the mariners of his boat sail round about, and he hath overthrown the fiend Apep.

FIRST PARTICIPANT: Hail, praise be unto thee, O thou who art as Ra who maketh himself to come into being in the form of the god Khepera.

SECOND PARTICIPANT: Hail, praise be unto thee, O thou who art as Ra, for he hath destroyed his enemies.

PRIESTESS: Hail, praise be unto Ra, for he hath crushed the heads of the children of impotent rebellion ...

Shake sistrum.

PRIEST: We give thanks to Ra, to Nut, to Geb, and to all the gods and goddesses who have helped us in this rite.

If the Sons of Horus, Qebhsennuf, Duamutef, Imsety and Hapi, have been called on for protection, they should be thanked too and bid farewell before dissolving the circle.

Shake sistrum.

SOURCES: *The Pyramid Texts*, Utterance 269, translation by RO Faulkner. *The Book of the Dead*, Chapters 137B and 140, translation by EA Wallis Budge. 'The Seventy-Five Praises of Ra', translation by EA Wallis Budge in *The Gods of the Egyptians*. Hymn to Nut from *Myth and Symbol in Ancient Egypt*, translation by RT Rundle Clark. Hymn to Nut from the Mummy of Soutywes in the Louvre, quoted by Anne Baring and Jules Cashford in *The Myth of the Goddess*.

Spring Equinox
21–22 March

As already mentioned, the seasons in Egypt, on account of the flooding of the Nile, were virtually the reverse of our experience. The resurrection of Osiris and the erection of the Djed-pillar would therefore have occurred at the beginning of winter for the Egyptians. For the rites in this book, we have split the celebrations concerning Osiris into two parts: the rite marking his death is left at the correct date (the Celtic Samhain, festival of the dead, at the end of October or beginning of November), while the rite marking his resurrection (which for the Egyptians would also have been celebrated in November), is here allocated to the spring, where it makes sense in terms of British seasons.

According to the myth, Osiris and his wife Isis were king and queen of Egypt in the First Time, when the *neteru* lived on earth. It was the Golden Age, for Isis and Osiris taught the people all the arts of civilization, and thus raised them out of a condition of savagery.

Everyone loved Osiris, because he was so kind and wise. After he had civilized Egypt, he travelled all over the world to teach people in other countries. He never used force to persuade them to give up their barbaric ways, but won them over by entertaining them with educational songs. His sister Nephthys, who was married to their brother Set, desired Osiris. As she was the twin of Isis, she managed to pass herself off as Isis in order to trick Osiris into having an affair with her. As a result of this liaison, she conceived the god Anubis, but tried to conceal this from Set by abandoning the baby after he was born. Fortunately for Anubis, he was brought up in the desert by wild dogs, which is why he is represented in the form of a dog or jackal.

Perhaps it was because of this act of adultery that Set became murderously jealous of Osiris. There are two versions of what he did. Native Egyptian sources refer to his taking the form of a wild boar and goring or trampling Osiris to death before pushing him into the Nile, at a place called Nedit, meaning 'where he was cast down'. The location is also called Gehesty. In the other version, recorded by Plutarch, Set tricked Osiris into climbing inside an ornate chest which he offered at a party as a prize for whomever its dimensions fitted best, having deliberately made it to Osiris's measurements and having ensured that the seventy-two other guests at the party (who were co-conspirators) were a different shape and size. When Osiris was inside, Set and his helpers closed the lid, sealed it, and threw the chest into the Nile so that Osiris drowned. It seems likely that this story of the body floating along the Nile relates to the apparent drift of the constellation of Orion, regarded as Osiris, along the Milky Way, as the stars seem to change their position slightly, day by day.

Isis and Nephthys recovered the body; but in the version of the story according to Plutarch, Isis found that it had washed up against the river bank at Byblos, where a tree had grown around it which was later used as a pillar to support the roof of the palace of the king and queen of that land, Syria. Isis had to remove the pillar before she could recover the body of her husband. It seems that this version of the story may have been an explanation of why Osiris was associated with the Djed-pillar – a fertility symbol resembling a stylized tree, which was erected in a ceremony at the start of the planting season. A wall painting of the pharaoh Seti I in his temple at Abydos, depicting him raising the pillar with the help of Isis (or a priestess in the role of the goddess), shows that the original Djed was taller than a man. Miniature versions, representing the 'backbone of Osiris', were placed on the bodies of the dead during the mummification process, to lend the deceased the quality of stability in the afterlife.

At the ceremony of erecting the Djed-pillar, a girdle or skirt was tied around the pillar. This girdle was associated with the Tet Knot or 'Buckle of Isis', which could be represented in an amulet made of carnelian, a red stone, placed for protection on the bodies of the dead. The Tet was identified with the blood of Isis (possibly menstrual blood, as the source of her magical power). To tie a girdle in the form of a Tet Knot (a bow) around the Djed-pillar symbolized the sexual union of Isis and Osiris. Rows of alternating Djeds and Tets were used as decorative borders in Egyptian religious art to symbolize the male and female divine principles in harmony. In the myth, Isis raises Osiris up from the dead by means of her magic, and keeps him alive long enough to make love to him and conceive their son Horus.

After this, Osiris leaves the earth to reign in Amenti, the underworld – the realm of the dead.

There is a sense in which Osiris is always alive, even though he is dead, because he is continually dying and being resurrected within the cycles of nature. As well as being associated with plant life, he is also the god of the moon, which wanes and waxes. (Thoth and Khonsu are also moon gods, but according to the Egyptian way of thinking, there is no inconsistency in this.) In one version of the myth, while Set is out hunting by the light of the full moon, he discovers Osiris's body where Isis has hidden it. He dismembers it into fourteen parts and scatters them all over Egypt, so that Isis, Nephthys and Anubis have to go in search of the pieces and reassemble the body. The fourteen parts could be seen as representing the fourteen pieces 'removed' from the moon during the fourteen nights of its waning, when it appears to get smaller and smaller; and these pieces are 'replaced' during the fourteen nights of the waxing part of the moon's cycle, as Isis and Nephthys restore their brother's body. Easter Day, the celebration of Jesus's resurrection, is on the first Sunday after the first full moon after the vernal equinox. It would therefore be very appropriate to celebrate the resurrection of Osiris on Easter Day, or on the day of the full moon before Easter, as an alternative to performing the rite on the day of the equinox itself.

In the texts in this rite, Osiris is shown as the indwelling divine principle in many aspects of nature: the earth, the sun, the sea, the Nile in flood, and the vegetation, particularly the crops which provide food. Above all, he is the potential for life, hidden in the dark earth, which appears dead in the barren season but which is ready to bring forth new growth when the fertile season returns.

To perform this rite, you will need a small Djed-pillar. It is fairly simple to make one from the cardboard tube taken from the inside of a roll of kitchen paper. A Djed-pillar has four flanges at its upper end. To make these, you will need to cut out four discs of cardboard, each about four inches in diameter. Cut three sections, each of about an inch and a quarter, off the end of the tube, and insert three of the cardboard discs between these sections, gluing them in place. Glue the last disc onto the end to make the top flange. (It is easier to assemble if you glue each section onto the middle of a disc and wait for it to dry, then glue the parts together, one on top of another, to complete the pillar.) If you like, the top can be finished off by gluing on the cap from a small jar. A slightly larger lid could also be fixed to the base, to give it more stability. The pillar should then be painted (with acrylic paint) in suitable spring colours, such as green and yellow. In the section between the second and third flange, you could paint some Utchat eyes – a pair on each side, so that they may be seen from both directions.

A few names and concepts which appear in this rite need to be explained. 'Inert One', 'Bull of Djedu', 'Lord of the West', 'Helpless One' and 'Listless One' are titles of Osiris. Un-nefer, 'the good being', is another of his epithets. Isis is described as the Wailer because she takes the form of a kite – a small bird of prey – when she mourns Osiris; a 'screecher' is another such bird. The Djendru bark is a deified boat. Shen-a-sek is a sea. The Mansion of the Prince in On is the palace of divine justice in Heliopolis. Thoth is spoken of as the son of Osiris in one of the texts, because Osiris is often identified with Ra, as at the end of the rite, in the Priestess's final speech. The White

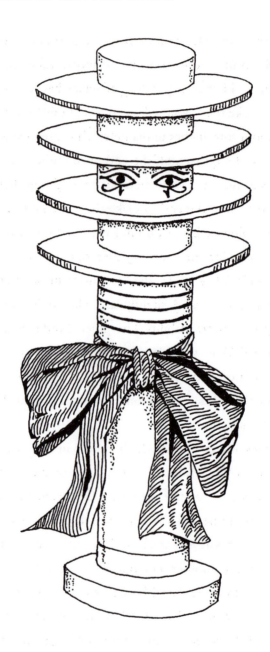

A Djed-pillar made from a cardboard tube

Crown, *hedjet*, is the pharaonic crown of Upper Egypt. The Per-nu is one of two national shrines: it was in the Delta, under the protection of the goddess Wadjet, here identified with Isis. The Hau-nebut are the Isles. Har-Sopd is Horus identified with the falcon god Sopdu of the eastern Delta region. Ra-Harmachis is the Sphinx. Atmu is a god of the primeval waters. Horus, rather confusingly, is referred to as if he is already adult, even though he has yet to be born at this stage of the myth; but in the timeless realm of the *neteru*, this way of thinking makes sense, since Horus is a divine principle which is eternally present.

In this rite there is a very brief assumption of the godform of Set by the First Participant. This may make some people uneasy; but it should be remembered that Set is not a totally evil deity, and was once worshipped like any other god: the pharaohs called Seti were named in his honour. So long as the godform departs fully at the end of the rite – something which should always be ensured, regardless of the type of godform that is assumed – then there is no danger to the participants. Some people speak as if Set were the Egyptian equivalent of the Devil, but this is far from being the case: he is a divine principle, albeit a stormy and impetuous one.

The Resurrection
of Osiris

Cast the circle in the usual way and, if desired, call on Qebhsennuf in the East, Duamutef in the South, Imsety in the West and Hapi in the North for protection.

Two candles on the altar are unlit at start of rite. Incense is also unlit. A model of a Djed-pillar lies on its side, with a red ribbon beside it. The Priestess has a sistrum.

Shake sistrum.
Light the candles.

FIRST PARTICIPANT: The shining Eye of Horus cometh. The brilliant Eye of Horus cometh. It cometh in peace, it sendeth forth rays of light unto Ra in the horizon, and it destroyeth the powers of Set, according to the decree. It leadeth them on and it taketh possession of him, and its flame is kindled against him. Its flame cometh and goeth about, and bringeth adoration; it cometh and goeth about heaven in the train of Ra upon the two hands of thy two sisters, O Ra. The Eye of Horus liveth, yea liveth.

Light the incense.

SECOND PARTICIPANT:
The fire is laid, the fire shines;
The incense is laid on the fire, the incense shines.
Your perfume comes to us, O Incense;
May our perfume come to you, O Incense:
Your perfume comes to us, you gods;
May our perfume come to you, you gods;
May we be with you, you gods;
May you be with us, you gods.
May we live with you, you gods;
May you live with us, you gods.
We love you, you gods;
May you love us, you gods.

Shake sistrum.

PRIEST: Hail to you, Lady of Goodness, at seeing whom those [who] are in the Netherworld rejoice, who removes the limpness of the Inert One, because of whom Osiris has trodden, who made for him the stride of those who walk in his moment of interment, in this your name of 'Dam which is under the feet'.

Hail to you, Mistress of the Old Ones, Lady of many faces in the Secret Place, who gives orders to the Bull of Djedu, who guides the Lord of the West, at whom Osiris rejoiced when he saw her; Mistress of the hidden mysteries, who announces festivals in the bow of the bark when men navigate in the morning, to whom the Inert One has turned his face in this her name of Mistress of Faces.

Hail to you, Great One behind your lord; who raises him up after being limp ...

Hail to you, you who are in attendance on your lord, Mourner of Osiris, the Great One, the Wailer, Mistress of the Per-nu ...

PRIESTESS:
The beneficent Isis who protected her brother
    and sought for him, she would
take no rest until she had found him.
She shaded him with her feathers and gave him air
    with her wings.
She cried out for joy and brought her brother to land.
She revived the weariness of the Listless One and took his
    seed into her body,
thus giving him an heir.
She suckled the child in secret, the place where he was
    being unknown.

PRIEST: Hail to you, you tree which encloses the god, under which the gods of the Lower Sky stand, the end of which is cooked, the inside of which is burnt, which sends out the pains of death: may you gather together those who are in the Abyss, may you assemble those who are in the celestial expanses. Your top is beside you for Osiris when the Djed-pillar of the Great One is loosed, like her who presides over Hetepet who bows to the Lord of the East. Your tomb, O Osiris, your shade which is over you, O Osiris, which repels your striking-power, O Set; the peaceful maiden who helped this spirit of Gehesty; your shadow, O Osiris.

FIRST PARTICIPANT: The Djed-pillar of the Day-bark is released for its lord, the Djed-pillar of the Day-bark is released for its protector. Isis comes and Nephthys comes, one of them from the west and one of them from the east, one of them as a 'screecher', one of them as a kite; they have found Osiris, his brother Set having laid him low in Nedit; when Osiris said 'Get away from me', when his name became Sokar.

PRIESTESS AS ISIS:
Ah Helpless One!
Ah Helpless One asleep! Ah Helpless One in this place
    which you know not – yet I know it!
Behold I have found you lying on your side –
    the great Listless One.
Ah, Sister!

PRIEST: Says Isis to Nephthys.

PRIESTESS AS ISIS:

This is our brother,

Come let us lift up his head,

Come let us rejoin his bones,

Come let us reassemble his limbs,

Come let us put an end to all his woe,

    that, as far as we can help, he will weary no more.

May the moisture begin to mount for this spirit!

May the canals be filled through you!

May the names of the rivers be created through you!

Osiris, live!

Osiris, let the great Listless One arise!

I am Isis.

SECOND PARTICIPANT AS NEPHTHYS:

I am Nephthys,

It shall be that Horus will avenge you,

It shall be that Thoth will protect you

   – your two sons of the Great White Crown –

It shall be that the Company will hear,

Then will your power be visible in the sky

    and you will cause havoc among the hostile gods,

      for Horus, your son, has seized the Great White Crown –

      seizing it from him who acted against you.

Then will your father Atum call 'Come!'

Osiris, live!

Osiris, let the great Listless One arise!

PRIEST: The sky reels, the earth quakes, Horus comes, Thoth appears, they raise Osiris from upon his side and make him stand up in front of the Two Enneads. Remember, Set, and put in your heart this word which Geb spoke, this threat which the gods made against you in the Mansion of the Prince in On because you threw Osiris to the earth, when you said, O Set:

FIRST PARTICIPANT AS SET: I have never done this to him.

PRIEST: So that you might have power thereby, having been saved, and that you might prevail over Horus; when you said, O Set:

FIRST PARTICIPANT AS SET: It was he who attacked *me*.

PRIEST: When there came into being this his name of 'Earth attacker'; when you said, O Set:

FIRST PARTICIPANT AS SET: It was he who kicked *me*.

PRIEST: When there came into being this his name of Orion, long of leg and lengthy of stride, who presides over Upper Egypt.

Raise yourself, O Osiris, for Set has raised himself, he has heard the threat of the gods who spoke about the god's father. Isis has your arm, O Osiris; Nephthys has your hand, so go between them. The sky is given to you, the earth is given to you, and the Field of Rushes, the Mounds of Horus, the Mounds of Set; the towns are given to you and the nomes assembled for you by Atum, and he who speaks about it is Geb.

PRIESTESS: Rise up thou, O Osiris. Thou hast thy backbone, O Still-Heart, thou hast the ligatures of thy neck and back, O Still-Heart. Place thou thyself upon thy base. I put water beneath thee, and I bring unto thee a Djed of gold that thou mayest rejoice therein.

The Djed-pillar is stood upright. Shake sistrum.

SECOND PARTICIPANT: O Osiris the King, arise, lift yourself up! Your mother Nut has borne you, Geb has wiped your mouth for you, the Great Ennead protects you and has put for you your foe under you.

ALL: Carry one who is greater than you.

FIRST PARTICIPANT: Say they to him in your name of 'Palace of the Great Saw'.

ALL: Lift up him who is greater than you.

FIRST PARTICIPANT: Say they in your name of 'Thinite Nome'. Your two sisters Isis and Nephthys come to you that they may make you hale, and you are complete and great in your name of 'Wall of the Bitter Lakes', you are hale and great in your name of 'Sea'; behold, you are great and round in your name of 'Ocean'; behold, you are circular and round as the circle which surrounds the Hau-nebut; behold, you are round and great as Shen-a-sek.

SECOND PARTICIPANT: Isis and Nephthys have waited for you in Asyut, and because their god is in you in your name of 'God'; they praise you lest you be far from them in your name of 'Sacred Beard'; they join you lest you be angry in your name of 'Djendru-bark'.

PRIESTESS: Your sister Isis comes to you rejoicing for love of you. You have placed her on your phallus and your seed issues into her, she being ready as Sothis, and Har-Sopd has come forth from you as Horus who is in Sothis.

The red ribbon is tied in a bow around the Djed-pillar, to represent the union of Isis and Osiris. Shake sistrum.

FIRST PARTICIPANT: It is well with you through him in his name of 'Spirit who is in the Djendru-bark', and he protects you in his name of Horus, the son who protects his father.

Shake sistrum.

PRIESTESS: Hail, thou lord of the underworld, thou Bull of those who are therein, thou image of Ra-Harmachis, thou Babe of beautiful appearance, come thou to us in peace. Thou didst repel thy disasters, thou didst drive away evil hap; Lord, come to us in peace.

SECOND PARTICIPANT: O Un-nefer, lord of food, thou chief, thou who art of terrible majesty, thou God, president of the gods, when thou dost inundate the land all things are engendered.

PRIEST: Thou art gentler than the gods. The emanations of thy body make the dead and the living to live, O thou lord of food, thou prince of green herbs, thou mighty lord, thou staff of life, thou giver of offerings to the gods, and of sepulchral meals to the blessed dead.

FIRST PARTICIPANT: Thy soul flieth after Ra, thou shinest at dawn, thou settest at twilight, thou risest every day; thou shalt rise on the left hand of Atmu for ever and ever.

PRIESTESS: Thou art the glorious one, the vicar of Ra; the company of the gods cometh to thee invoking thy face, the flame whereof reacheth unto thine enemies. We rejoice when thou gatherest together thy bones, and when thou hast made whole thy body daily.

SECOND PARTICIPANT: Anubis cometh to thee, and the two sisters come to thee. They have obtained beautiful things for thee, and they gather together thy limbs for thee, and they seek to put together the mutilated members of thy body. Wipe thou the impurities which are on them upon our hair and come to us having no recollection of that which hath caused thee sorrow.

PRIEST: Come thou in thy attribute of 'Prince of the Earth', lay aside thy trepidation and be at peace with us, O Lord. Thou shalt be proclaimed heir of the world, and the One god, and the fulfiller of the designs of the gods. All the gods invoke thee, come therefore to thy temple and be not afraid.

Shake sistrum.
Meditation.
Shake sistrum.

PRIESTESS: O Ra, thou art beloved of Isis and Nephthys; rest thou in thy habitation for ever.

PRIEST: We give thanks to Osiris, to Isis, to Nephthys, to Horus, to Thoth, to the Spirit of the Sacred Tree, and to all the deities who have helped us in this rite.

If the Sons of Horus, Qebhsennuf, Duamutef, Imsety and Hapi, have been called on for protection, they should be thanked too and bid farewell, before dissolving the circle.
Shake sistrum.

SOURCES: *The Pyramid Texts*, Utterances 269, 366, 477, 532 and 574, translation by RO Faulkner. *The Coffin Texts*, Spells 236, 238 and 239, translation by RO Faulkner. *The Book of the Dead*, Chapters 137B and 155, translation by EA Wallis Budge. 'The Lamentations of Isis and Nephthys' (*Coffin Texts*, Spell 74) and an XVIIIth Dynasty Hymn to Osiris, both from *Myth and Symbol in Ancient Egypt*, translation by RT Rundle Clark. 'The Songs of Isis and Nephthys' from the Bremner-Rhind Papyrus, translation by EA Wallis Budge in *Egyptian Religion*.

Beltane: 1 May

The festival of Hathor of Dendera and Horus of Edfu in mid-May celebrated their wedding. In Britain, the wedding of the Goddess and God is traditionally at the fertility festival of May Day on 1 May, so we have allocated this rite of Hathor and Horus to that date.

Horus of Edfu was Horus the Elder, Haroeris, the brother of Osiris, Isis, Nephthys and Set. However, he was often identified with his nephew, Horus the Younger, Harpocrates, the son of Isis and Osiris. We have therefore taken the liberty of using a text at the end of this rite which refers to Horus the Younger, because it is very appropriate in other respects in that it applies to his aspect as lord of food and provider of abundance. The opening hymn is addressed to the sun god as Harakhti, Horus of the Horizon, who, in this case, is the rising sun. (Sometimes Harakhti is also the constellation of Leo, as we shall see in the Lughnasad rite.)

In ancient Egypt, the festival of Hathor and Horus was celebrated by taking the cult statue of Hathor, the goddess of love and beauty, from her temple in Dendera, with great ceremony along the Nile in a barge called *Mistress of Love*, to visit her husband Horus in his temple at Edfu. The goddess's boat was accompanied by five others carrying important officials, whilst people who wished to join the procession followed in small boats behind, or by foot along the banks of the river. On the way, there were stops at Karnak, Komir, and Hierakonopolis Nekhen, for various rituals to be undertaken. When the procession reached Edfu, an act of divination was performed, in which four geese, representing the Four Sons of Horus, were released to fly to the four cardinal points: if they flew the wrong way, it was regarded as a bad omen. Provisions were distributed among the ordinary people to enable them to celebrate to the full, and it was a time of great jubilation. Musicians, singers and dancers joined in the joyful rites, and this was when the Hymn to the Golden One, which is included in this Beltane rite, was sung. The entire festival lasted for a month, from the full moon to the full moon.

Hathor, whose name means 'house of Horus' (that is, the sky, the place where the sun dwells), is both a lunar and a solar goddess, as indicated by her headdress of lunar (cow's) horns and solar disc; but in her marriage to Horus the sun god, her lunar aspect would have been emphasized. The texts that are incorporated in this rite show her to be a formidable deity. In her hymn, she is identified with Neith, the warlike creator goddess of Sais, and also with Isis, Egypt's foremost goddess.

The sistrum, as explained before, is a ceremonial rattle sacred to Hathor: it was often decorated on both sides with her cow-eared human face, representing the positive and negative aspects of the goddess as Isis and Nephthys. The Pelican, mentioned in the rite, is a goddess regarded as the mother of the dead, who prophesies a safe passage for them through the underworld. The Sistrum-player is a priest or son of Hathor. The Two Ladies of Dep are the goddesses Wadjet and Nekhbet – the *uraeus* (cobra) and vulture emblems on the pharaoh's crown. Wadjet, the *uraeus* goddess of Lower Egypt, was from an early time identified with Isis. Edjo, a name of Hathor, was another name for Wadjet. Nekhbet, the vulture goddess of Upper Egypt, was sometimes identified with Hathor. Hathor is also the Eye of Horus (or the Eye of Ra), which was identified with the mother goddess Mut, mentioned in the hymn. This Eye was the sun itself, and her fierce destroyer form is Sekhmet. Tefnut, mentioned in the hymn, like Sekhmet, is also depicted as a lioness. The *hamemet* in the Second Participant's final speech are celestial beings who may once have been human or may become so. 'Aten' is the name of the sun god conceived of as the solar disc.

The Festival of Hathor and Horus

Cast the circle in the usual way and, if desired, call on Qebhsennuf in the East, Duamutef in the South, Imsety in the West and Hapi in the North for protection.

Two candles on the altar are unlit at start of rite. Incense is also unlit. The Priestess has a sistrum.

Shake sistrum.

Light the candles.

FIRST PARTICIPANT: The shining Eye of Horus cometh. The brilliant Eye of Horus cometh. It cometh in peace, it sendeth forth rays of light unto Ra in the horizon, and it destroyeth the powers of Set, according to the decree. It leadeth them on and it taketh possession of him, and its flame is kindled against him. Its flame cometh and goeth about, and bringeth adoration; it cometh and goeth about

heaven in the train of Ra upon the two hands of thy two sisters, O
Ra. The Eye of Horus liveth, yea liveth.

Light the incense.

SECOND PARTICIPANT:

The fire is laid, the fire shines;

The incense is laid on the fire, the incense shines.

Your perfume comes to us, O Incense;

May our perfume come to you, O Incense:

Your perfume comes to us, you gods;

May our perfume come to you, you gods;

May we be with you, you gods;

May you be with us, you gods.

May we live with you, you gods;

May you live with us, you gods.

We love you, you gods;

May you love us, you gods.

Shake sistrum.

PRIEST:

May you wake in peace, O Purified, in peace!

May you wake in peace, O Horus of the East, in peace!

May you wake in peace, O Soul of the East, in peace!

May you wake in peace, O Harakhti, in peace!

May you sleep in the Night-bark,

May you wake in the Day-bark,

For you are he who oversees the gods,

There is no god who oversees you!

PRIEST: The Pelican prophesies, the Shining One goes forth, the dress of Hathor is woven, a path is prepared for me that I may pass by. I know his path, even of him who is skilled in his movements, one whose face is hidden from those who see him.

PRIESTESS: The Sistrum-player is in my body, the pure flesh of my mother, and the dress will enclose me. I don the dress of Hathor, my hands are under it to the width of the sky, my fingers are under it as living uraei, my nails are under it as the Two Ladies of Dep, and I kiss the earth, I worship my mistress, for I have seen her beauty; I give praise to Hathor, for I have seen her beauty.

FIRST PARTICIPANT: I give her the dress, her shape is distinguished above those of the gods, and I see her beauty. She creates the fair movements which I make when the Protector of the land comes; the gods come to me bowing and praise is given to me by the gods, they see me at my duty, and I am initiated into what I did not know; I cross with the retinue of this Great Lady to the western horizon of the sky, I speak in the Tribunal.

SECOND PARTICIPANT AS A HORIZON DWELLER: This path of yours; whence is this path of yours?

FIRST PARTICIPANT: Say the horizon dwellers to me.

I have come here from the river-bank of Her on my ascents of the Mountain of the sehseh-bird, so that I may don the cloak of this Great Lady who is in the bow of the bark of Ra and in the middle of the bark of Khepera. I found her when she repeated her manifestation and trebled her faces, her Serpent of Terror being on her brow, and her shape is distinguished above those of the gods ...

Shake sistrum.

PRIEST:

All hail, jubilation to you, O Golden One ...

Sole ruler, Uraeus of the Supreme Lord himself!

Mysterious one, who gives birth to the divine entities,

   forms the animals, models them as she pleases,

   fashions men ...

SECOND PARTICIPANT:

O Mother! ... Luminous One

   who thrusts back the darkness,

   who illuminates every human creature with her rays,

Hail Great One of many names ...

You from whom the divine entities come forth

   in this your name of Mut-Isis!

FIRST PARTICIPANT:

You-who-cause-the-throat-to-breathe,

daughter of Ra,

whom he spat forth from his mouth in this your name

of Tefnut!

PRIEST: O Neith who appeared in your bark in this your name of

Mut!

FIRST PARTICIPANT:

O Venerable Mother, you who subdue your adversaries

   in this your name of Nekhbet!

SECOND PARTICIPANT:

O You-who-know-how-to-make-right-use-of-the-heart,

   you who triumph over your enemies in this your name

   of Sekhmet!

PRIEST:

It is the Golden One ... the lady of drunkenness,

   of music, of dance,

   of frankincense, of the crown of young women,

   whom men acclaim because they love her!

PRIESTESS AS HATHOR: I am Hathor who brings her Horus and

who proclaims her Horus; and my heart is the lion-god ... there is no

limit to my vision, there are none who can encircle my arms, every god will take himself off before me. I have appeared as Hathor, the Primeval, the Lady of All, who lives on truth, who lifts up the faces of all the gods, and all the gods are beneath my feet. I am She who displays his beauty and assembles his powers, I am that Eye of Horus, the female messenger of the Sole Lord, the like of whom shall not be again. Truly I am She who made his name. I have flourished, I came into being before the sky was fashioned, and it gives me praise; before the earth was released and it exalts me, while I seek your saliva and your spittle; they are Shu and Tefnut. I have searched and sought out, and see, I have fetched what I sought; come with my horns and display my beauty; come with my face and I will cause you to be exalted. I have smitten all with my hands in this my name of Hathor; I have given my tears. I reduce them to order in this my name of She who is over reducing to order; I make warmth for them in this my name of Shesmetet. Such am I; I am Edjo, I am indeed the Mistress of the Two Lands.

Shake sistrum.
Meditation.
Shake sistrum.

PRIEST:
It is the Gold of the divine entities, who comes forth
    at her season,
    in the month of Epiphi, the day of the new moon,
    at the festival of 'She is delivered' ...

Heaven makes merry, the earth is full of gladness,

the castle of Horus rejoices.

FIRST PARTICIPANT: Horus has found his true voice; the rank of his father has been given to him. He has come forth crowned by the command of Geb. He has received the sceptre of the two lands; the White Crown is established upon his head. He judges the earth according to his plan; heaven and earth are under the seat of his face.

SECOND PARTICIPANT: He commands men, spirits, the dead, the hamemet, and Egypt, the lords of the earth, the region of Aten, are under his plans; the north wind, the flood, the celestial waters, the staff of life, every herb.

PRIEST: Nepra, he gives his green herbs; the lord of food, he leads on abundance – he gives it in the lands. Everywhere is joy: hearts are glad, hearts rejoice, every face is happy. Every place adores his beauties.

PRIESTESS: Doubly sweet his love is to us: his goodness goes round hearts. Great is his love in every body, and they do what is right to the son of Isis.

Shake sistrum.

PRIEST: We give thanks to Hathor, to Horus and to all the deities who have helped us in this rite.

If the Sons of Horus, Qebhsennuf, Duamutef, Imsety and Hapi, have been called on for protection, they should be thanked too and bid farewell before dissolving the circle.

Shake sistrum.

SOURCES: *The Pyramid Texts*, Utterances 269 and 573, translation by RO Faulkner. *The Coffin Texts*, Spells 331 and 484, translation by RO Faulkner. *The Book of the Dead*, Chapter 137B, translation by EA Wallis Budge. An XVIIIth Dynasty Hymn to Osiris from the Paris Stele in the Bibliothèque Nationale, based on the transliteration by EA Wallis Budge in *The Gods of the Egyptians*. Hymn to the Golden One from *Egyptian Mysteries* by Lucie Lamy, after the French translation by M Alliot.

Summer Solstice:
21–22 June

At this time of the year, the sun is at the height of its powers, as the days are long and the nights short. It seemed obvious, therefore, to make this rite a celebration of the powers of the sun, both as a god and as a goddess.

In the opening invocations, the sun god is addressed as Tem-Heru-khuti, the deity in his setting aspect, and as Ra, and Heru-khuti, 'Horus of the Two Horizons'. His mother is named as Hathor, who is also his daughter, but who, as a form of the sky goddess (Nut), gives birth to him each day. His father is Nu, the god of the primeval waters of chaos, the Nun, who features again later in the rite. 'Aukert' is another name for the underworld, and the Lake of Testes is presumably a heavenly, spiritual region.

There then follows a telling of the myth of the Destruction of Mankind, who were punished for blasphemy and rebellion against Ra, who sent Hathor/Sekhmet against them. The ambiguous character of this goddess is indicative of the Egyptian experience of the sun: the life-giving power, which makes the plants grow and on which all life on earth ultimately depends, may also be the death-dealing heat of the desert and drought. Such a powerful goddess must be regarded with love, awe, fear and deep respect, for people wished to enjoy her beneficent aspect and not her wrathful one. We now also discover why Hathor was referred to in the hymn in the Beltane rite as the lady of drunkenness!

Sekhmet-Bast-Ra is described by EA Wallis Budge as a form of Mut. Her depiction in the *Book of the Dead* shows her as a winged woman with a phallus. It seems clear, however, that this deity is an amalgam of goddess and god. The goddess Bast, or Bastet, is a benign form of Sekhmet. According to myth, when Sekhmet came back after running amok, Thoth, god of wisdom, calmed her down, and the raging lioness was gradually transformed, whilst returning home, into the sweet-natured cat, Bast! Sekhmet-Bast-Ra, then, would seem to be the sun in its fierce and benevolent forms, both female and male.

The 'living souls who are in their chests', 'great ones who are languid' and 'those who are in their caverns' are the dead, whom the goddess protects and restores to life. It is made apparent here that she also guards the Boat of Millions of Years (the boat of the sun) from the attacks of the Fiend, Apep, also called Nak.

The Eight gods, or Ogdoad, are a group of gods similar to the Ennead. The Sekhtet or Semktet (meaning 'becoming weak') boat is the Boat of Millions of Years in its aspect for the second half of the day, from midday to midnight. For the other twelve hours of the day, from midnight to midday, the Atet or Matet (meaning 'becoming strong') boat performs this function.

The Eye of Ra

Cast the circle in the usual way and, if desired, call on Qebhsennuf in the East, Duamutef in the South, Imsety in the West and Hapi in the North for protection.

Two candles on the altar are unlit at start of rite. Incense is also unlit. The Priestess has a sistrum.

Shake sistrum.
Light the candles.

FIRST PARTICIPANT: The shining Eye of Horus cometh. The brilliant Eye of Horus cometh. It cometh in peace, it sendeth forth rays of light unto Ra in the horizon, and it destroyeth the powers of Set, according to the decree. It leadeth them on and it taketh possession of him, and its flame is kindled against him. Its flame cometh and goeth about, and bringeth adoration; it cometh and goeth about

heaven in the train of Ra upon the two hands of thy two sisters, O Ra. The Eye of Horus liveth, yea liveth.

Light the incense.

SECOND PARTICIPANT:

The fire is laid, the fire shines;

The incense is laid on the fire, the incense shines.

Your perfume comes to us, O Incense;

May our perfume come to you, O Incense:

Your perfume comes to us, you gods;

May our perfume come to you, you gods;

May we be with you, you gods;

May you be with us, you gods.

May we live with you, you gods;

May you live with us, you gods.

We love you, you gods;

May you love us, you gods.

Shake sistrum.

PRIESTESS: Homage to thee, O thou glorious Being, thou who art dowered with all attributes, O Tem-Heru-khuti, when thou risest in the horizon of heaven, a cry of joy cometh forth to thee from the mouth of all peoples. O thou beautiful Being, thou dost renew thyself in thy season in the form of the Disk within thy mother Hathor; therefore in every place every heart swelleth with joy at thy rising forever.

PRIEST: The regions of the North and South come to thee with homage, and send forth acclamations at thy rising in the horizon of heaven; thou illuminest the two lands with rays of turquoise light. O Ra, thou who art Heru-khuti, the divine man-child, the heir of eternity, self-begotten and self-born, king of earth, prince of the Tuat, governor of the regions of Aukert; thou comest forth from the water, thou hast sprung from the god Nu, who cherisheth thee and ordereth thy members.

FIRST PARTICIPANT: O thou god of life, thou lord of love, all men live when thou shinest; thou art crowned king of the gods. The goddess Nut doeth homage unto thee, and Maat embraceth thee at all times.

SECOND PARTICIPANT: Those who are in thy following sing unto thee with joy and bow down their foreheads to the earth when they meet thee, thou lord of heaven, thou lord of earth, thou king of Right and Truth, thou lord of eternity, thou prince of everlastingness, thou sovereign of all the gods, thou god of life, thou creator of eternity, thou maker of heaven wherein thou art firmly established.

PRIESTESS: The company of the gods rejoice at thy rising, the earth is glad when it beholdeth thy rays; the peoples that have been long dead come forth with cries of joy to see thy beauties every day. Thou goest forth each day over heaven and earth and art made strong each day by thy mother Nut. Thou passest through the heights of heaven, thy heart swelleth with joy; and the Lake of Testes is content thereat.

Shake sistrum.

PRIESTESS: Ra was the god who created himself. After he was in sovereignty over humanity, gods and creation, the One, men and women were blaspheming, saying:

FIRST PARTICIPANT: Behold, his Majesty – life, strength, health – has grown old. His bones are silver, his limbs are gold, his hair is real lapis-lazuli.

SECOND PARTICIPANT: His Majesty was listening to what humanity said. Said his Majesty – life, strength, health – to those who were in his train:

PRIEST AS RA: Call – bring me my Eye, and Shu, Tefnut, Geb, Nut, and the father and mother gods who lived with me when, behold, I was in Nu, together with my god Nu. Let him bring his ministers with him. Bring them in silence, that humanity may not see; their hearts may not flee. Come with them into the great temple. Let them declare their counsel fully. I will enter into Nu, to the place where I was born. Let there be brought to me these gods.

PRIESTESS: These gods were on both sides of him, bowing to the earth before his Majesty. He spoke words before the father of the firstborn gods, the maker of humanity, the king of rational beings. They said before his Majesty:

Qebhsennuf, Hapi, Imsety and Duamutef, the Four Sons of Horus, guardian deities.

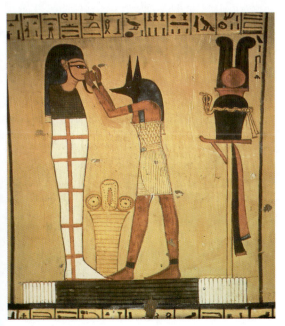

A masked priest of Anubis performs the Opening of the Mouth ceremony on a mummy, to restore the deceased to life in the next world.

Horus of Edfu.

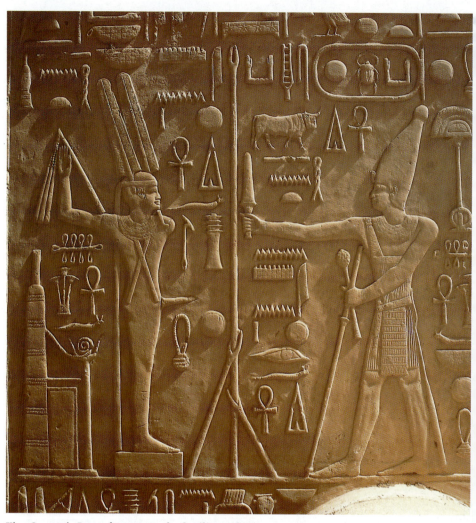

King Sesostris I pays homage to the fertility god Min.

Hathor, goddess of love and beauty, greets King Horemheb. Harsiese is on the right.

Thoth, the god of wisdom.

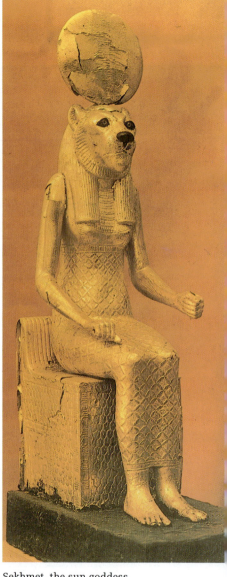

Sekhmet, the sun goddess.

Bast, goddess of joy and fertility.

Osiris as judge of the dead. His green skin symbolizes his resurrection in the plant life.

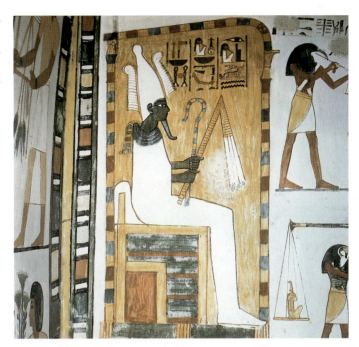

The sky goddess Nut swallows the sun each evening.

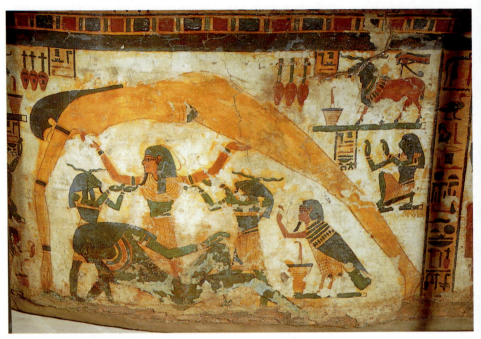

The air god Shu, aided by two ram gods, separates the sky goddess Nut from the earth god Geb.

Tutankhamun's pendant in the form of a protective Wedjat Eye flanked by the vulture goddess Nekhbet and the serpent goddess Wadjet. The counterpoise is in the form of two djed-pillars and a tet knot.

The Holy Family:
Horus and Isis
support Osiris
on his pillar.

Nephthys and
Isis support
Osiris-Ra in the
form of a ram.

Hor-em-Akhet, the Great Sphinx of Giza.

FIRST PARTICIPANT: Speak to us, for we are listening to them.

SECOND PARTICIPANT: Said Ra to Nu:

PRIEST AS RA: O firstborn god, from whom I came into being, and you ancestor gods, take heed of humanity who came into being from my Eye – they speak words against me. Tell me what you would do about it. Take heed of it for me. Seek out a plan for me. I will not slay them until I hear what you say about it.

PRIESTESS: Said the Majesty of Nu, son of Ra:

FIRST PARTICIPANT AS NU: God greater than he who made him, mightier than those who were created with him, sit on your throne. Great is the fear of you. Let your Eye be upon those who blaspheme you.

SECOND PARTICIPANT: Said the Majesty of Ra:

PRIEST AS RA: Behold them fleeing into the mountain. Their hearts are afraid because of what they have said.

PRIESTESS: They said before his Majesty:

SECOND PARTICIPANT AS A MOTHER GODDESS: Let your Eye go forth: let it destroy for you those who blaspheme in wickedness. Not an eye can better it in resistance when it goes down in the form of Hathor.

FIRST PARTICIPANT: Went forth then this goddess. She slew mankind on the mountain.

SECOND PARTICIPANT: Said the Majesty of this god:

PRIEST AS RA: Come – come in peace, Hathor, for the deed is done.

FIRST PARTICIPANT: Said this goddess:

PRIESTESS AS HATHOR-SEKHMET: You gave me life. When I had power over humanity, it was pleasing to my heart.

SECOND PARTICIPANT: Said the Majesty of Ra:

PRIEST AS RA: I will be master over them, as the king destroying them.

SECOND PARTICIPANT: It came to pass that Sekhmet of the offerings of the night waded about in their blood, beginning in Suten-henen. Said Ra:

PRIEST AS RA: Call – bring me messengers swift, speedy. They shall run like the shadow of the body.

FIRST PARTICIPANT: One brought these messengers straight away. Said the Majesty of this god:

PRIEST AS RA: Let them go to Elephantine – bring me mandrakes in great number.

PRIESTESS: One brought him these mandrakes. The Majesty of this god gave these mandrakes to Sektet, who is in Heliopolis, to crush. Behold, when women were bruising barley for beer and they were placing these mandrakes in the beer vessels, they became human blood.

SECOND PARTICIPANT: There having been made seven thousand vessels of beer, came therefore the Majesty of the king of the South and North, Ra, with these gods, to see this beer. Behold, when it was dawn, after the goddess had slaughtered humanity in their season of sailing up the river, said the Majesty of Ra:

PRIEST AS RA: It is good, it is good. I am for protecting humanity against her.

FIRST PARTICIPANT: Said Ra:

PRIEST AS RA: Let them carry and bring them to the place where she slew humanity.

SECOND PARTICIPANT: Commanded the Majesty of the king of the South and North, Ra, during the beauties of the night, to cause to be poured out these vases of sleep-inducing beer. The fields of the four heavens were filled with liquid by the will of the Majesty of this god.

PRIESTESS: Came this goddess in the morning. She found this place flooded. Joyful was her face because of it. She was drinking; merry was her heart. She came to a state of drunkenness. She did not know humanity.

   Said the Majesty of Ra to this goddess:

PRIEST AS RA: Come – come in peace, beautiful one.

FIRST PARTICIPANT: There came into being beautiful young women in Ament.

   Said the Majesty of Ra to this goddess:

PRIEST AS RA: Let there be made for her vases of sleep-inducing beer, at these seasons of the year: they shall be in proportion to my handmaidens.

SECOND PARTICIPANT: There were made vases of sleep-inducing beer according to the number of handmaidens of the festival of Hathor, by all mankind since the first day.

   Shake sistrum.

SECOND PARTICIPANT: Homage to thee, O Sekhmet-Bast-Ra, thou mistress of the gods, thou bearer of wings, lady of the Anes bandlet, queen of the crown of the South and of the North, only One, sovereign of her father, superior to whom the gods cannot be, thou mighty one of enchantments in the Boat of Millions of Years, thou who art pre-eminent, who risest in the seat of silence, mother of Pashakasa, royal wife of Parehaqa-Kheperu, mistress and lady of the tomb, mother in the horizon of heaven, gracious one, beloved, destroyer of rebellion, offerings are in thy grasp, and thou art standing in the bows of the boat of thy divine father to overthrow the Fiend. Thou hast placed Maat in the bows of his boat. Thou art the fire goddess Amit, whose opportunity escapeth her not ...

PRIEST: Praise be to thee, O lady, who art mightier than the gods, and words of adoration rise to thee from the Eight gods. The living souls who are in their chests praise thy mystery. O thou who art their mother, thou source from whom they sprang, who makest for them a place of repose in the hidden underworld, who makest sound their bones and preservest them from terror, who makest them strong in the abode of everlastingness, who preservest them from the evil chamber of the souls of the god-of-the-terrible-face who is among the company of the gods.

PRIESTESS AS HATHOR-ISIS: I am a net-snake, a soul in the bark 'Ordainer of power'. I am mistress of the oar in the Bark of Governance. I am the mistress of life, the serpent-guide of the sunshine on fair paths. I am she who strengthens the lashings on the steering-oars on the western ways. I am the third one, mistress of brightness, who guides the great ones who are languid on the paths of the wakeful. I am the mistress of splendour on the paths of the cloudy sky. I am mistress of the winds on the Island of Joy. I am the mistress of strength who guides those who are in their caverns. I am

Hathor, mistress of the northern sky, who strengthened the bonds of the wakeful on that night when the earth quaked and seksut was among the mourners. I am Isis whom Nut bore, who displays her beauty, who puts together her power and who lifts up Ra to the Daybark.

Shake sistrum.
Meditation.
Shake sistrum.

PRIEST: Ra liveth by Maat the beautiful. The Sekhtet boat draweth on and cometh into port; the South and the North, the West and the East turn to praise thee, O thou primeval substance of the earth who didst come into being of thine own accord.

FIRST PARTICIPANT: Isis and Nephthys salute thee, they sing unto thee songs of joy at thy rising in the boat, they protect thee with their hands.

SECOND PARTICIPANT: The souls of the east follow thee, the souls of the west praise thee.

PRIESTESS: Thou art the ruler of all the gods, and thou hast joy of heart within thy shrine, for the serpent fiend Nak hath been condemned to the fire, and thy heart shall be joyful for ever.

Shake sistrum.

PRIEST: We give thanks to Ra, to Hathor, to Sekhmet, to Sekhmet-Bast-Ra, to Isis, to Nu, and to all the deities who have helped us in this rite.

If the Sons of Horus, Qebhsennuf, Duamutef, Imsety and Hapi, have been called on for protection, they should be thanked too and bid farewell before dissolving the circle.

Shake sistrum.

SOURCES: *The Pyramid Texts*, Utterance 269, translation by RO Faulkner. *The Coffin Texts*, Spell 332, translation by RO Faulkner. *The Book of the Dead*, Chapters 137B and 164, translation by EA Wallis Budge. Hymn to Ra from *The Papyrus of Nekht*, Sheet 21, Document 10,471 in the British Museum, translation by EA Wallis Budge in *The Book of the Dead*. The Legend of Sekhmet from the tombs of Seti I and Rameses IV at Thebes, based on the transliteration by EA Wallis Budge in *The Gods of the Egyptians*.

9

Lughnasad:
1 August

ughnasad is the Celtic harvest festival, also called Lammas, Loaf Feast, because it is the celebration of the grain harvest. For the Egyptians, of course, the grain harvest was in the spring. In August, however, an event occurs which was extremely important for the Egyptians: this is the heliacal rise of Sirius – its rise just before dawn. As it is the star of Isis, this signifies the return of the goddess after her long search for her dead husband. Now she has found him, as the constellation of Orion. During the summer, Orion and Sirius are in the sky during the day time, so are not visible; their reappearance was a time for rejoicing – even more so because it happened to coincide with the flooding of the Nile, which fertilized the land. The occasion was seen as the birthday of the gods, and was the Egyptian New Year. When Egyptian civilization was at its height, the heliacal rise of Sirius would have been at the summer solstice, but because of the precession of the equinoxes, it occurred later and later in the year, and is now in August.

In this rite, we have combined the Heliopolitan Creation myth, about the origin of the gods, with a text which, according to Bauval and Hancock in *Keeper of Genesis*, is part of a rite performed on the plain of Giza, called Rostau by the Egyptians, in honour of the gods' birthday (which then, as explained, would have been at the summer solstice).

The rite opens by welcoming Ra: he is 'the god who reckoneth millions of years'. The Thigh is a constellation, probably the Great Bear. Next comes an invocation of Osiris and Isis as Orion and Sothis (Sirius). 'Bull of Nedit' and 'Bull of the West' are titles of Osiris. This is followed by the Book of Knowing the Evolutions of Ra, at the beginning of which he is called Neb-er-Tcher, the lord of the universe, and is identified with Osiris.

After this comes the text which refers to the rite which would have been performed at Rostau, 'the place more noble than any place', in front of the Great Sphinx. Bauval and Hancock have convincingly demonstrated that the Great Sphinx, known to the Egyptians as Hor-em-Akhet – 'Horus *in* the horizon' – is the earthly representation of Harakhti – 'Horus *of* the horizon' – which is the constellation of Leo. Hor-em-Akhet and Harakhti were also identified with Ra. If the revised dating of the Sphinx is correct, it could well have been constructed in the Age of Leo (10,500 BC is the date given by Bauval and Hancock), when the sun would have been rising in the constellation of Leo at the vernal equinox: facing east, the Sphinx would have been gazing towards its celestial counterpart as the sun rose between Leo's paws. Centuries later, in 2,500 BC, at the time when the pyramids of Giza were built, this event would have occurred at the summer solstice.

To the Egyptian way of thinking, the land of Egypt mirrored the heavens, with the Nile corresponding to the Milky Way. The pharaoh, who was the earthly equivalent of the sun, Horus, ritually enacted its movements in an earthly parallel to celestial events, crossing the Nile by boat and approaching the Sphinx, his journey corresponding to the path of the sun (the ecliptic) crossing the Milky Way during the seventy days when Sirius is absent from the night sky. On the day when the heliacal (dawn) rising of Sirius occurred (the summer solstice in those days), the pharaoh would stand immediately in front of the Sphinx, just as the sun was in conjunction with Regulus, the star on the breast of Leo, regarded as the 'star of kings'. Thus would earthly events exactly correspond to heavenly events.

It seems that the pyramids at Giza represent the stars in Orion's belt (as shown in *The Orion Mystery* by Adrian Gilbert and Robert Bauval), and so the whole area may be regarded as the earthly body of Osiris, 'when his name became Sokar' (the falcon-headed god of the dead). As the place of Osiris on earth, it therefore corresponds to the Tuat, his place in the sky as Orion. According to Bauval and Hancock, Giza could also be the place of the First Time, the primeval mound on which the Creator stood perhaps being the very outcrop of rock on which the Great Pyramid is built!

On the gods' birthday, the pharaoh would have been challenged by priests in front of the Sphinx, asking him which of the two routes he would take into the Tuat: one on water, the other on land. It may be that there were actual physical versions of these – a stone causeway and an underground flooded tunnel from the Sphinx to the pyramids, which may have been used in initiation rituals.

In this Lughnasad rite, there are a few terms which need explanation. The Wag festival is at the beginning of August. The mention of splitting open the eyes and mouth of the Inert One (Osiris) is a reference to the Opening of the Mouth ritual performed for the dead to ensure that they would possess all their senses and faculties in the afterlife. Aker, mentioned at the end of the Creation story, is an earth god, represented as a lion with two front parts, who guards the gates of the underworld. The Lake of Sehseh is presumably an otherworldy location, as is Iasu. The concept of having one's 'mouth equipped' applies to having esoteric knowledge and being able to utter the correct words of power in the correct way when required.

The Creation and Birth of the Gods

Cast the circle in the usual way and, if desired, call on Qebhsennuf in the East, Duamutef in the South, Imsety in the West and Hapi in the North for protection.

Two candles on the altar are unlit at start of rite. Incense is also unlit. The Priestess has a sistrum.

Shake sistrum.
Light the candles.

FIRST PARTICIPANT: The shining Eye of Horus cometh. The brilliant Eye of Horus cometh. It cometh in peace, it sendeth forth rays of light unto Ra in the horizon, and it destroyeth the powers of Set, according to the decree. It leadeth them on and it taketh possession of him, and its flame is kindled against him. Its flame cometh and goeth about, and bringeth adoration; it cometh and goeth about

heaven in the train of Ra upon the two hands of thy two sisters, O Ra. The Eye of Horus liveth, yea liveth.

Light the incense.

SECOND PARTICIPANT:
The fire is laid, the fire shines;
The incense is laid on the fire, the incense shines.
Your perfume comes to us, O Incense;
May our perfume come to you, O Incense:
Your perfume comes to us, you gods;
May our perfume come to you, you gods;
May we be with you, you gods;
May you be with us, you gods.
May we live with you, you gods;
May you live with us, you gods.
We love you, you gods;
May you love us, you gods.

Shake sistrum.

PRIEST: The heavens are opened, the earth is opened, the West is opened, the East is opened, the southern half of heaven is opened, the northern half of heaven is opened, the doors are opened, and the gates are thrown wide open to Ra as he cometh forth from the horizon. The Sektet boat openeth for him the double doors and the Matet boat bursteth open for him the gates; he breatheth, and the god Shu cometh into being, and he createth the goddess Tefnut. Those who are in the following of Osiris follow in his train ...

PRIESTESS: Hymns of praise be unto you, O ye divine beings of the Thigh, the knives of God work in secret, and the two arms and hands of God cause the light to shine; it is doubly pleasant unto him to lead the old unto him along with the young at his season. Now, behold, the god Thoth dwelleth within his hidden places, and he performeth the ceremonies of libation unto the god who reckoneth millions of years, and he maketh a way through the firmament, and he doeth away with storms and whirlwinds from his stronghold ...

FIRST PARTICIPANT: Hymns of praise unto thee, O Ra, in the horizon, and homage unto thee, O thou that purifiest with light the denizens of heaven, O thou who hath sovereign power over heaven at that supreme moment when the paddles of thine enemies move with thee!

Shake sistrum.

PRIESTESS: Behold, he has come as Orion, behold, Osiris has come as Orion, Lord of Wine in the Wag-festival.

SECOND PARTICIPANT AS NUT: My beautiful one!

PRIESTESS: Said his mother.

FIRST PARTICIPANT AS GEB: My heir!

PRIESTESS: Said his father of him whom the sky conceived and the dawn-light bore ... He who lives, lives by the command of the gods, and you live. You will regularly ascend [as] Orion from the eastern region of the sky, you will regularly descend [as] Orion into the western region of the sky, your third is Sothis pure of thrones, and it is she who will guide you ... on the goodly roads which are in the sky in the Field of Rushes.

PRIEST: Hail to you, Lady of offerings, at whom Osiris rejoices when he sees her, whose great wall is an owner of possessions; who brings air, who gives offerings, who presides over the throne in the secret places of the Netherworld; who clears the vision of the Bull of Djedu, who split open his mouth and split open his eyes when the Inert One asked; who gathered together his arms and legs, who laid Osiris down ... who gave abundance to the Lord of the Flood on the desert plateau; who gave offerings.

SECOND PARTICIPANT: All the lower portions of the god's-offerings have come to [us], even the due of Her who is behind her lord, the Companion of the Bull of Nedit who makes his body to breathe, who veils the limpness, who spiritualizes the Bull of the West, to whom Osiris has turned his back, helper of Anubis.

FIRST PARTICIPANT: The Book of Knowing the Evolutions of Ra, of overthrowing Apep. The words of Neb-er-Tcher. He says:

PRIEST AS RA: I became the Creator of what came into being. I came into being in the forms of Khepera, coming into being in the First Time ... I became the Creator of what came into being, that is, I produced myself from primordial matter I made ... My name is Osiris, primordial matter of primordial matter. I have done all my will in this earth. I have spread abroad in it ...

I brought into my mouth my own name – that is, a word of power. I, even I, came into being as the things which came into being, and I came into being in the forms of Khepera. I came into being from primordial matter, coming into being in multitudes of forms from the beginning. No created things existed in this land: I made everything whatsoever that was made. I was alone: there existed no other who worked with me in that place. I made what I made there by means of a divine soul that I raised there from Nu, from an inert state. I did not find a place where I could stand. I performed a spell in my heart: I laid a foundation before me. I made everything whatsoever that was made. I was alone: I laid a foundation in my heart. I made other things which came into being – multitudes of things which came into being of Khepera ...

I, even I, spat out Shu; I emitted Tefnut. I became, from one god, three gods – that is, from me two gods came into being on this earth ...

I collected my members: they came forth from me after I had sexual union with my fist. My heart came to me out of my hand. The semen which fell into my mouth I spat in the form of Shu. I emitted water as Tefnut. I became, from one god, three gods ... Were raised up Shu and Tefnut in Nu where they were ...

Plants and reptiles came from the god Rem, from the tears from me. My Eye wept: humanity came into being. I endowed it with power. It raged against me after it came, finding another growth in its place. Its vigorous power fell upon its bushes, upon the bushes I placed there to adorn it. Ruling, therefore, on its seat in my face, it rules the whole earth.

Shu and Tefnut gave birth to Nut, Osiris, Heru-khenti-an-maati, Set, Isis, Nephthys. Behold their children: they create multitudes of beings on earth – this from the beings of children from the beings of their children. They invoke my name; they overthrow their enemies; they create words of power for the overthrow of Apep, who is to be bound by the two hands of Aker.

Shake sistrum.

PRIESTESS:
The reed-floats of the sky are set down for Ra
  by the Day-bark
That Ra may cross on them to Harakhti at the horizon.
The reed-floats of the sky are set down for Harakhti
  by the Night-bark
That Harakhti may cross on them to Ra at the horizon.
The reed-floats of the sky are brought down to me
  by the Day-bark
That I may go up on them to Ra at the horizon.
The reed-floats of the sky are brought down to me
  by the Night-bark
That I may go up on them to Harakhti at the horizon.

FIRST PARTICIPANT: I go up on this eastern side of the sky where the gods were born, and I am born as Horus, as Him of the Horizon; I am vindicated and my double is vindicated; Sothis is my sister, the Morning Star is my offspring. I have found the spirits with their mouths equipped, who sit on the shores of the Lake of Sehseh, the drinking-bowl of the spirit whose mouth is an owner of equipment.

SECOND PARTICIPANT AS ONE OF THE SPIRITS: Who are you?

FIRST PARTICIPANT: Say they to me, say the spirits with their mouths equipped.
   I am a spirit with his mouth equipped.

SECOND PARTICIPANT AS THE SPIRIT: How has this happened to you ...

FIRST PARTICIPANT: Say they to me, say the spirits with their mouths equipped.

SECOND PARTICIPANT AS THE SPIRIT: That you have come to this place more noble than any place?

FIRST PARTICIPANT: I have come to this place more noble than any place because:

PRIEST:

The reed-floats of the sky were set down for Ra
  by the Day-bark
That Ra might cross on them to Harakhti at the horizon.

PRIESTESS:

The reed-floats of the sky were set down
  for Harakhti by the Night-bark
That Harakhti might cross on them to Ra at the horizon.

FIRST PARTICIPANT:

The reed-floats of the sky were brought
  down to me by the Day-bark
That I might go up on them to Ra at the horizon.

SECOND PARTICIPANT:

The reed-floats of the sky were brought
  down to me by the Night-bark
That I might go up on them to Harakhti at the horizon.

PRIEST: I go up on this eastern side of the sky where the gods were born, and I am born as Horus, as Him of the Horizon; I am vindicated and my double is vindicated, so acclaim me and acclaim my double, for Sothis is my sister, the Morning Star is my offspring.

SECOND PARTICIPANT: I will come with you and wander with you in the Field of Rushes; I will serve as herdsman with you in the

Field of Turquoise; I will eat of what you eat, I will live on what you live on, I will be clad in that with which you are clad, I will be anointed with that with which you are anointed, I will take water with you from the Nurse-canal, the drinking-bowl of the spirit whose mouth is the owner of equipment.

PRIESTESS: I sit at the head of the Great Conclave and give orders to the spirit whose mouth is the owner of equipment; I sit on the bank of the Lake of Sehseh and give orders to the spirit whose mouth is the owner of equipment.

Shake sistrum.
Meditation.
Shake sistrum.

PRIESTESS: Hail to you, O Ra, in your life and in your beauty, in your thrones, in your [gold]. Bring [us] the milk of Isis, the flood of Nephthys, the overspill of the lake, the surge of the sea, life, prosperity, health, happiness, bread, beer, clothing, and food, that [we] may live thereby. May [we] see you when you go forth as Thoth, when a waterway is prepared for the Bark of Ra to his fields which are in Iasu; may you rush on as one who is at the head of his Chaos-gods.

Shake sistrum.

PRIEST: We give thanks to Ra, Neb-er-Tcher, to Osiris, to Harakhti, to Isis, to Nut, to Geb, to the spirits with their mouths equipped, and to all the deities who have helped us in this rite, and we thank them for the harvest and for all of life's blessings which they have given to us.

If the Sons of Horus, Qebhsennuf, Duamutef, Imsety and Hapi, have been called on for protection, they should be thanked too and bid farewell before dissolving the circle.

Shake sistrum.

SOURCES: *The Pyramid Texts*, Utterances 269, 406, 442 and 473, translation by RO Faulkner. *The Coffin Texts*, Spells 238 and 241, translation by RO Faulkner. *The Book of the Dead*, Chapter 137B, translation by EA Wallis Budge. 'The Book of Knowing the Evolutions of Ra' from Papyrus number 10,188 in the British Museum, based on the transliteration by EA Wallis Budge in *The Gods of the Egyptians*.

10

Autumnal Equinox: 21–22 September

At the autumnal equinox, the powers of the sun are on the wane: day and night are the same length, as they are at the vernal equinox. The autumnal equinox marks the beginning of the darkest months of the year, when night prevails over day. Not until the winter solstice, when the sun is 'reborn', do the days begin to grow longer.

The Legend of Ra and Isis seems to allude to this time of year. It is a strange story, which has puzzled some commentators who have speculated that it may have been written at a time when the cult of Isis was in the ascendancy and Ra had fallen from favour; but this explanation has been largely rejected. In any case it does not take into account the mythic quality of the story and the fact that Pagan myths generally relate to natural phenomena.

In the story, Ra is senile – the sun in the declining part of the year. He comes down to earth and drools on the ground – an image of the sun at sunset. The events therefore would seem to take place on an autumn evening. Isis uses Ra's own power against him in the form of a serpent – that symbol which, as we have seen, is usually associated with his solar Eye, the essence of his potency. Yet the solar Eye is also Isis herself in her identification with Hathor/Sekhmet. Isis compels Ra to yield up his two eyes, the sun and the moon, to her and her son Horus, who is another, younger, form of the sun god, to be born at the winter solstice. What at first appears to be a tale of trickery and betrayal is actually about renewal and regeneration. At the end of the story, Ra is restored to health, and his powers are shared with his great granddaughter and great great grandson, thus ensuring the perpetual continuity of the solar and lunar principles.

The Legend of Ra and Isis was used as a spell against snake bite, as explained in Chapter 3. It provides an excellent example of ancient Egyptian attitudes to magic, including the power of the name and the use of images in magic. Isis uses a familiar method, making a psychic link with her victim by means of a substance from his body (in this case, saliva, but any bodily substance will do) which she uses to animate the image of the serpent. Animated by his power, it is really an aspect of himself – probably his Eye, which is a goddess in its own right. His name, his *ren*, is identified with his heart, the essence of himself. Once Isis knows the secret of the Divine Name, she can perform powerful magic and command the poison to leave Ra's body.

At the end of this rite, there is an offering to Min, an ithyphallic fertility god whom the Greeks identified with Pan. The ancient Egyptian harvest festival, which was in the spring, was dedicated to Min. The pharaoh would visit the god's shrine to make offerings, then accompany his cult statue in a grand procession. The statue of Min was then set up on a ceremonial platform called his 'staircase', in a field, and the pharaoh would reap the first ears of wheat and present them to the god. It may be that the pharaoh and his queen then performed a rite of sexual union. Finally, four sparrows were released to the four cardinal points.

Although Min was an important deity, connected to the cult of the pharaoh, surprisingly little is known about him. Some egyptologists think that he may have been simply the fertility aspect of Amun, and not a distinct *neter* at all. Certainly Min became identified with Horus, and in this guise, his mother was Isis. There was also a goddess of the harvest, Renenutet, a serpent-headed deity later assimilated to Isis. Isis was therefore regarded sometimes as the mother and sometimes as the consort of Min.

A few words in this rite need to be explained. A *henti* period is 60 years, so a double *henti* period is 120 years. Temu is the ageing sun god, and Heru-hekennu is a hawk-headed god, worshipped in Bubastis as the offspring of Bast and Osiris. Meht-urt is a cow goddess of the sky. 'Bull of his Mother' is a title of Horus.

The Legend of Ra and Isis and the Harvest of Min

Cast the circle in the usual way and, if desired, call on Qebhsennuf in the East, Duamutef in the South, Imsety in the West and Hapi in the North for protection.

Two candles on the altar are unlit at start of rite. Incense is also unlit. The Priestess has a sistrum. There is bread, or cakes or biscuits, and wine or an alternative drink, sufficient for everyone present.

Shake sistrum.

Light the candles.

FIRST PARTICIPANT: The shining Eye of Horus cometh. The brilliant Eye of Horus cometh. It cometh in peace, it sendeth forth rays of light unto Ra in the horizon, and it destroyeth the powers of Set, according to the decree. It leadeth them on and it taketh possession of him, and its flame is kindled against him. Its flame cometh and goeth about, and bringeth adoration; it cometh and goeth about heaven in the train of Ra upon the two hands of thy two sisters, O Ra. The Eye of Horus liveth, yea liveth.

Light the incense.

SECOND PARTICIPANT:
The fire is laid, the fire shines;
The incense is laid on the fire, the incense shines.
Your perfume comes to us, O Incense;
May our perfume come to you, O Incense:
Your perfume comes to us, you gods;
May our perfume come to you, you gods;
May we be with you, you gods;
May you be with us, you gods.
May we live with you, you gods;
May you live with us, you gods.
We love you, you gods;
May you love us, you gods.

Shake sistrum.

PRIESTESS: May I be joined unto Isis the divine lady, and may she protect me from him that would do an injury unto me ...

PRIEST: Chapter of the god divine, self-produced, maker of heaven, earth, the breath of life, fire, gods, men, beasts, cattle, creeping things, birds and fish, the king of men and gods, in one form, to whom double henti periods are as years – one with many names. Unknown is that god, not known to the gods.

SECOND PARTICIPANT: Behold, Isis was as a woman skilled in words. Her heart rebelled at the millions of men: she chose rather the millions of the gods; she esteemed the millions of the spirits. Could she not be in heaven and earth like Ra, make herself mistress of the earth, a goddess (she meditated in her heart) by knowing the name of the holy god?

FIRST PARTICIPANT: Behold, came Ra every day, at the front of his sailors, and was established on the throne of the two horizons. He had become old, the divine one: he dribbled at his mouth; he poured out emissions on the ground, and his spittle fell on the earth.

SECOND PARTICIPANT: Isis, she kneaded it in her hand with earth which was on it. She fashioned it into a sacred serpent. She made it in the form of a dart. It did not move along alive before her. She left it lying on the path whereon journeyed the great god, according to his desire, through his Two Lands.

FIRST PARTICIPANT: The god holy rose up. Behind, the gods in the great double house (life, strength, health) were following him. He marched on as he did every day. The sacred serpent bit him. The fire of life was coming out from him: it devastated the dweller in the cedars.

SECOND PARTICIPANT: The god divine, he opened his mouth. The voice of his Majesty (life, strength, health) reached to heaven. The gods were saying:

ALL, AS THE GODS: What is it?

SECOND PARTICIPANT: His gods were saying:

ALL, AS THE GODS: What is the matter?

FIRST PARTICIPANT: He did not find words to answer about it. His two jaws rattled; his limbs all trembled; the poison took possession of his body as the Nile takes possession of his river bed.

SECOND PARTICIPANT: The great god established his heart. He cried out to those in his train:

PRIEST AS RA: Come to me, you who have come into being from my members, gods who have proceeded from me, and I will make you know what has happened. I am wounded by something deadly – my heart knows it. My eyes have not seen it; my hand made it not. I do not know anyone who has done this to me. I have not tasted pain like it. Never was anything more deadly than it. I am a prince, the son of a prince – the divine issue produced by a god. I am a great one, the son of a great one. My father thought out my name. I am of many names, many forms: my form is living in every god. I have proclaimed Temu and Heru-hekennu. My father and my mother have uttered my name: it was hidden in my body by my begetter who wished not to let him who would enchant me have power by enchantments over me. I had come forth from the abode to see what I had made – was being led through the lands I created – when something aimed a blow at me. I know not what it is. Behold, it is not fire; behold, it is not water. My heart contains fire; my limbs are trembling; my members contain the children of quakings. I pray you, let there be brought to me my children, the gods mighty of words, skilful with their mouths – their powers, they reach to heaven.

FIRST PARTICIPANT: Came to him his children – every god there, with his cries of weeping. Came Isis with her power – her skilled mouth with the breath of life. Her incantations destroy diseases: her words make rotting throats live. Said she:

PRIESTESS AS ISIS: What is this, father god? What is it? A snake has shot sickness into you? A thing made by you has lifted up its head against you? Verily it shall be overthrown by beneficent words of power. I will make it depart from the sight of your rays.

SECOND PARTICIPANT: The god holy opened his mouth:

PRIEST AS RA: I was passing over the way, going through the Two Lands of my country. My heart wished to see what I had created. I was bitten by an invisible snake. Behold, it is not fire; behold, it is not water. I am colder than water; I am hotter than fire. All my limbs are full of sweat; I tremble; my eye is without stability. I cannot see heaven: water bursts out on my face, as in summer.

FIRST PARTICIPANT: Said Isis to Ra:

PRIESTESS AS ISIS: O tell me your name, father god. The person lives who has declared his name.

PRIEST AS RA: I am the maker of heaven and earth, the knitter together of the mountains, the creator of what exists upon it. I am the maker of water, bringing into existence Meht-urt, the maker of the Bull of his Mother, the creator of the pleasures of love. I am the maker of heaven and have covered the two horizons. I have set the soul of the gods within them. I am he who opens his eyes and the light comes into being, who shuts his eyes and the darkness comes into being. The flood of Hapi rises when he gives the command. The gods do not know his name. I am the maker of hours, the creator of days. I am the opener of the festivals of the year, the creator of streams of water. I am the maker of the flame of life, causing works to be per-formed in houses. I am Khepera in the morning, Ra in his noontide, Temu in the evening.

SECOND PARTICIPANT: The poison was not driven from its course: the great god was not relieved. Said Isis to Ra:

PRIESTESS AS ISIS: Your name is not included among the things which you have said to me. O tell it to me and out shall come the poison. The person shall live, having uttered his name.

FIRST PARTICIPANT: The poison, it burned with burnings: it was stronger than the flame of fire. Said the Majesty of Ra:

PRIEST AS RA: I give myself to be searched out by Isis. My name shall come forth from my body into her body.

SECOND PARTICIPANT: The divine one hid himself from the gods. Empty was the seat in the boat of millions of years.

FIRST PARTICIPANT: When it became nearly the time of the coming forth of the heart, she said to her son Horus:

PRIESTESS AS ISIS: Let him bind himself by an oath on the life of the god that the god will give his two eyes.

SECOND PARTICIPANT: The great god had his name removed from him.

FIRST PARTICIPANT: Isis, great in words of power, said:

PRIESTESS AS ISIS: Run out, poison: come forth from Ra! Eye of Horus, come forth from the god and shine outside his mouth! I – I have worked! I make the poison which is defeated fall down on the ground! Verily was his name removed from the great god! Ra, may he live: the poison, may it die! The poison, may it die: Ra, may he live! ...

SECOND PARTICIPANT: Thus said Isis, Great Lady, mistress of the gods, who knew Ra by his own name.

Shake sistrum.
Meditation.
Shake sistrum.

The following three speeches are to be spoken over the food and drink before it is shared between the people present. A portion should be left as an offering to the god Min himself, and may be deposited on the earth out of doors, after the rite.

PRIESTESS:
I worship Min, I extol arm-raising Horus:
Hail to you, Min in his procession!
Tall-plumed, son of Osiris,
Born of divine Isis.

PRIEST:
Great in Senut, mighty in Ipu,
You of Coptus, Horus strong-armed,
Lord of awe who silences pride,
Sovereign of all the gods!

PRIESTESS:

Fragrance laden when he comes from Medja-land,

Awe inspiring in Nubia,

You of Utent, hail and praise!

The food and drink are consumed. Reports of the meditation experience may be exchanged at this point, if desired.

Shake sistrum.

PRIEST: We give thanks to Ra, to Isis, to Min, and to all the gods and goddesses who have helped us in this rite, and we give thanks to Min for the harvest which provides our sustenance.

If the Sons of Horus, Qebhsennuf, Duamutef, Imsety and Hapi, have been called on for protection, they should be thanked too and bid farewell before dissolving the circle.

Shake sistrum.

SOURCES: *The Pyramid Texts*, Utterance 269, translation by RO Faulkner. *The Book of the Dead*, Chapters 68 and 137B, translation by EA Wallis Budge. 'The Legend of Ra and Isis' from the Turin Papyrus, based on the transliteration by EA Wallis Budge in *The Gods of the Egyptians*. 'Hymn to Min', from Ancient Egyptian Literature volume 1, by Miriam Lichtheim.

11

Samhain: 31 October

The Celtic festival of Samhain is the Feast of the Dead. In Egypt, the Mysteries of Osiris, concerning his death and resurrection, took place in early November. For the Egyptians, as we already know, the beginning of winter was the time for ploughing and sowing, so had a different significance for them than for us. To cope with this, as already explained, we have divided the Mysteries of Osiris into two sections, placing the resurrection at the vernal equinox, but leaving his death at this festival of Samhain.

There are many similarities between this rite and the one for the vernal equinox, but we have left out the fertility aspects and emphasized the mourning and grief of Isis and Nephthys. The Lamentations of Isis and Nephthys, which features here, would actually have been sung in ancient times during the November ceremonies in honour of Osiris by two priestesses representing the goddesses.

Again, a few words which may be puzzling need to be explained. The terms 'Mourner of Osiris' and 'celestial serpent' apply to Isis. 'An' and 'Hunnu' are names for Osiris, identifying him with the sun god. 'Anpu' is the original Egyptian name for Anubis. Ptah–Seker or Ptah–Seker-Tem is the Creator god identified with the god of the dead. The souls of Pe are falcon gods associated with Horus and identified with the Ancestors. Osiris's 'eldest daughter' who is put in charge of guarding the imprisoned Set is a daughter of Ra – probably either Tefnut or Sekhmet. 'Heru-khuti with long strides' is Horus of the Two Horizons, but here may refer to Osiris as Orion. Akert is the underworld, and An-rut-f is a region in it. Suten-henen is the capital of Heracleopolis, a district (called a nome) of Egypt. Nekhen was an ancient city in Upper Egypt. Abtu is Abydos, the cult centre of Osiris. Wepwawet is a jackal or wolf deity closely resembling Anubis. In the litany of Osiris, the Second Participant refers to bringing Hapi forth from his source. This is the god of the Nile, represented as a corpulent man with pendulous breasts, and is not to be confused with the ape-headed Hapi who is one of the Four Sons of Horus.

The litany of Osiris from *The Book of the Dead* was read on behalf of the souls of the dead to ensure that they would be granted safe passage through the underworld to reach the Hall of the Double Maati and pass the test when their souls were weighed in the balance. We may therefore read this long prayer both for ourselves, that we may be helped in our path through life, and for the postmortem welfare of deceased loved ones whom we remember at this festival of Samhain.

The Mysteries of Osiris

Cast the circle in the usual way and, if desired, call on Qebhsennuf in the East, Duamutef in the South, Imsety in the West and Hapi in the North for protection.

Two candles on the altar are unlit at start of rite. Incense is also unlit. The Priestess has a sistrum.

Shake sistrum.
Light the candles.

FIRST PARTICIPANT: The shining Eye of Horus cometh. The brilliant Eye of Horus cometh. It cometh in peace, it sendeth forth rays of light unto Ra in the horizon, and it destroyeth the powers of Set, according to the decree. It leadeth them on and it taketh possession of him, and its flame is kindled against him. Its flame cometh and goeth about, and bringeth adoration; it cometh and goeth about

heaven in the train of Ra upon the two hands of thy two sisters, O Ra. The Eye of Horus liveth, yea liveth.

Light the incense.

SECOND PARTICIPANT:
The fire is laid, the fire shines;
The incense is laid on the fire, the incense shines.
Your perfume comes to us, O Incense;
May our perfume come to you, O Incense:
Your perfume comes to us, you gods;
May our perfume come to you, you gods;
May we be with you, you gods;
May you be with us, you gods.
May we live with you, you gods;
May you live with us, you gods.
We love you, you gods;
May you love us, you gods.

Shake sistrum.

PRIEST: Hail to you, Mourner of Osiris who bewails the limp Great One, who makes a spirit of the Bull of the West; at seeing whom the Westerners rejoice; Lady of All in the secret place; to whom Osiris turns his back in these his moments of inertness; who is in front of the Lord of Abydos; whose place on the paths of the Netherworld is hidden; who bewails her lord at the interment in this her name of 'She who bewails her lord' ...

Hail to you, Mourner of Osiris, Companion of the Bull of Nedit who makes the mummy-wrappings to breathe, who veils the limpness, to whom Osiris has turned his back, helper of the embalmer Anubis when treating the body of the Inert One ...

PRIESTESS: The glorious Isis was perfect in command and in speech, and she avenged her brother. She sought him without ceasing, she wandered round and round the earth uttering cries of pain, and she rested not until she had found him. She overshadowed him with her feathers, she made air with her wings, and she uttered cries at the burial of her brother.

PRIEST: ... The 'screecher' comes, the kite comes, namely Isis and Nephthys; they have come seeking their brother Osiris, seeking their brother the King ...

FIRST PARTICIPANT: Weep for your brother, O Isis; weep for your brother, O Nephthys; weep for your brother.

PRIEST: Isis sits down with her hands on her head, Nephthys has grasped the tips of her breasts because of their brother the King, who crouches on his belly, an Osiris in his danger, an Anubis foremost of grip.

FIRST PARTICIPANT: You shall have no putrefaction, O [Osiris]; you shall have no sweat, O [Osiris]; you shall have no efflux, O [Osiris]; you shall have no dust, O [Osiris] ...

PRIEST: The starry sky serves your celestial serpent whom you love
...You have relieved Horus of his girdle, so that he may punish the
followers of Set ...Your eyes have been given to you as your two uraei
because you are Wepwawet who is on his standard and Anubis who
presides over the God's Booth.

FIRST PARTICIPANT: Behold now, Isis speaketh:

PRIESTESS AS ISIS:
Come to thy house, Oh An!
Come to thy house for thine enemies are not!
Behold the excellent sistrum-bearer – come to thy house!
Lo, I thy sister, love thee – do not thou depart from me!
Behold Hunnu, the beautiful one!
Come to thy house immediately – come to thy temple immediately!
Behold thou my heart, which grieveth for thee;
Behold me seeking for thee – I am searching for thee
    to behold thee
Lo, I am prevented from beholding thee –
I am prevented from beholding thee, oh An! ...
I love thee more than all the earth –
And thou lovest not another as thou dost thy sister!

PRIEST: Behold now, Nephthys speaketh:

SECOND PARTICIPANT AS NEPHTHYS:

Behold the excellent

  sistrum-bearer! Come to thy house!

Cause thy heart to rejoice, for thy enemies are not!

All thy sister-goddesses are at thy side and behind

  thy couch,

    calling upon thee with weeping – yet thou art

    prostrate upon thy bed!

Hearken unto the beautiful words uttered by us

  and by every noble one among us!

Subdue thou every sorrow which is in the hearts of

  thy sisters,

Oh thou strong one among the gods,

  – strong among men who behold thee!

We come before thee, oh prince, our lord;

Turn thou not away thy face before us;

Sweeten our hearts when we behold thee, oh prince!

Beautify our hearts when we behold thee!

I, Nephthys, thy sister, I love thee:

Thy foes are subdued, there is not one remaining.

Lo, I am with thee; I shall protect thy limbs

  for ever, eternally.

PRIEST: Thy right eye is like the Sektet boat; thy left eye is like the Atet boat; thine eyebrows are like Anpu; thy fingers are like Thoth; thy hair is like Ptah-Seker; they make a fair way for thee, and they smite down for thee the fiends of Set.

PRIESTESS AS ISIS: I have come to protect thee, O Osiris, with the north wind which cometh forth from Tem; I have strengthened for thee thy throat; I have caused thee to be with the god; and I have placed all thine enemies under thy feet.

SECOND PARTICIPANT AS NEPHTHYS: I go round about behind my [brother Osiris]. I have come that I may protect thee, and my strength which protecteth shall be behind thee for ever and ever. The god Ra hearkeneth unto thy cry; thou, O [son of Nut], art made to triumph, thy head shall never be taken away from thee, and thou shalt be made to rise up in peace.

Shake sistrum.

FIRST PARTICIPANT: The doors of the sky are opened, the doors of the celestial expanses are thrown open; the gods who are in Pe are full of sorrow, and they come to Osiris the King at the sound of the weeping of Isis, at the cry of Nephthys, at the wailing of these two spirits over this great one who has come forth from the Netherworld. The souls of Pe clash sticks for you, they clap their hands for you, they tug their side-locks for you, they smack their thighs for you, and they say to you:

PRIEST AS A SOUL OF PE: O Osiris the King, you have gone, but you will return, you have slept, but you will awake, you have died, but you will live. Stand up and see what your son has done for you, wake up and hear what Horus has done for you. He has smitten for you him who smote you as an ox, he has slain for you him who slew you as a wild bull, he has bound for you him who bound you and has set him under your eldest daughter who is in Kedem, that mourning may cease in the Two Conclaves of the gods.

Shake sistrum.

PRIESTESS: Praise be unto thee, O Osiris, lord of eternity, Unnefer, Heru-khuti, whose forms are manifold, and whose attributes are majestic. Ptah-Seker-Tem in Annu, the lord of the hidden place, and the creator of Het-ka-Ptah and of the gods therein, the guide of the underworld, whom the gods glorify when thou settest in Nut. Isis embraceth thee in peace, and she driveth away the fiends from the mouth of thy paths. Thou turnest thy face upon Amentet, and thou makest the earth to shine as with refined copper. Those who have lain down rise up to see thee, they breathe the air and they look upon thy face when the disk riseth on its horizon; their hearts are at peace inasmuch as they behold thee, O thou who art Eternity and Everlastingness.

PRIEST: Homage to thee, O lord of starry deities in Annu, and of heavenly kings in Kher-aha; thou god Unti, who art more glorious than the gods who are hidden in Annu.

ALL: O grant thou unto me a path whereon I may pass in peace, for I am just and true; I have not spoken lies wittingly, nor have I done aught with deceit.

FIRST PARTICIPANT: Homage to thee, O An in Antes, Heru-khuti, with long strides thou stridest over heaven, O Heru-khuti.

ALL: O grant thou unto me a path whereon I may pass in peace, for I am just and true; I have not spoken lies wittingly, nor have I done aught with deceit.

SECOND PARTICIPANT: Homage to thee, O Soul of ever-lastingness, thou Soul that dwellest in Djedu; the Ureret crown is established upon thy head; thou art the One who maketh the strength which protecteth himself, and thou dwellest in peace in Djedu.

ALL: O grant thou unto me a path whereon I may pass in peace, for I am just and true; I have not spoken lies wittingly, nor have I done aught with deceit.

PRIESTESS: Homage to thee, O lord of the Acacia Tree, the Seker boat is set upon its sledge; thou turnest back the Fiend, the worker of evil, and thou causest the Utchat to rest upon its seat.

ALL: O grant thou unto me a path whereon I may pass in peace, for I am just and true; I have not spoken lies wittingly, nor have I done aught with deceit.

PRIEST: Homage to thee, O thou who art mighty in thine hour, thou great and mighty Prince, dweller in An-rut-f, lord of eternity and creator of everlastingness, thou art lord of Suten-henen.

ALL: O grant thou unto me a path whereon I may pass in peace, for I am just and true; I have not spoken lies wittingly, nor have I done aught with deceit.

FIRST PARTICIPANT: Homage to thee, O thou who restest upon Right and Truth, thou art the lord of Abtu, and thy limbs are joined unto Ta-tchesertet; thou art he to whom fraud and guile are hateful.

ALL: O grant thou unto me a path whereon I may pass in peace, for I am just and true; I have not spoken lies wittingly, nor have I done aught with deceit.

SECOND PARTICIPANT: Homage to thee, O thou who art within thy boat, thou bringest Hapi forth from his source; the light shinest upon thy body and thou art the dweller in Nekhen.

ALL: O grant thou unto me a path whereon I may pass in peace, for I am just and true; I have not spoken lies wittingly, nor have I done aught with deceit.

PRIEST: Homage to thee, O creator of the gods, thou King of the North and South, O Osiris, victorious one, ruler of the world in thy gracious seasons; thou art the lord of the celestial world.

ALL: O grant thou unto me a path whereon I may pass in peace, for I am just and true; I have not spoken lies wittingly, nor have I done aught with deceit.

Shake sistrum.

Meditation.

Shake sistrum.

PRIESTESS AS IMSETY: I am thy daughter, O [Osiris], and I have come to protect thee; I make thy house to germinate and to be stablished firmly according to what Ptah hath commanded and according to what Ra hath commanded.

PRIEST AS HAPI: I have come to protect thee, O [Osiris] ...; I bind up for thee thy head and thy members, I smite down thine enemies for thee beneath thee, and I give thee thy head for ever.

SECOND PARTICIPANT AS DUAMUTEF: I am thy daughter who loveth thee, O [Osiris] ...; I have come and I have avenged thee, O my father Osiris, upon him that did evil unto thee and I have brought him under thy feet.

FIRST PARTICIPANT AS QEBHSENNUF: I am Qebhsennuf, and I have come that I may protect [Osiris]; I have collected into a whole body for thee thy bones, and I have gathered together for thee thy members, I have brought thy heart and do set it upon its seat within thy body, and I make thy house to germinate after thee.

PRIEST: Osiris speaks to Horus, for he has removed the evil which was on the King on his fourth day, he has nullified what was done to him on his eighth day, and you have come forth from the Lake of

Life, having been cleansed in the Lake of Cool Water, and having become Wepwawet. Your son Horus guides you, he has given you the gods who are your foes, and Thoth brings them to you. How happy are those who see, how content are those who behold, even they who see Horus when he gives life to his father and extends his was-staff to Osiris in the face of the western gods!

FIRST PARTICIPANT: A libation for you is poured out by Isis, Nephthys has cleansed you, even your two great and mighty sisters who gathered your flesh together, who raised up your members, and who caused your eyes to appear in your head, namely the Night-bark and the Day-bark.

PRIESTESS: I have given Atum to you, I have made the Two Enneads for you, your children's children together have raised you up, namely Hapi, Imsety, Duamutef and Qebhsennuf, whose names you have wholly made. Your face is washed, your tears are wiped away, your mouth is split open with their iron fingers, and you go forth that you may go up to the broad hall of Atum, travel to the Field of Rushes, and traverse the places of the great god.

SECOND PARTICIPANT: The sky is given to you, the earth is given to you, the Field of Rushes is given to you; it is the two great gods who row you, even Shu and Tefnut, the two great gods of On. The god wakes, the god stands up because of the spirit which came forth from the Netherworld, even Osiris the King who came forth from Geb.

Shake sistrum.

PRIEST: We give thanks to Osiris, to Isis, to Nephthys, to Horus, to Qebhsennuf, to Duamutef, to Imsety and to Hapi, and to all the deities who have helped us in this rite.

If the Sons of Horus, Qebhsennuf, Duamutef, Imsety and Hapi, have been called on for protection, they should be thanked for this service too and bid farewell, before dissolving the circle.

Shake sistrum.

SOURCES: *The Pyramid Texts*, Utterances 269, 535 and 670, translation by RO Faulkner. *The Coffin Texts*, Spell 237, translation by RO Faulkner. *The Book of the Dead*, Chapters 137B and 151A, translation by EA Wallis Budge. An XVIIIth Dynasty Hymn to Osiris, translation by EA Wallis Budge in *Egyptian Religion*. A Hymn and Litany to Osiris from the Papyrus of Ani, Sheet 19, Document 10,470 in the British Museum, translation by EA Wallis Budge in *The Book of the Dead*. 'The Lamentations of Isis and Nephthys' from the Berlin Papyrus, from *The Burden of Isis*, translation by James Teackle Dennis, quoted by Anne Baring and Jules Cashford in *The Myth of the Goddess*.

12

Winter Solstice: 21–22 December

Long before Christians celebrated Christmas, the winter solstice was the time of the rebirth of the sun god as the solar child. In Egypt and throughout the Graeco-Roman world, 25 December was the birthday of Harpocrates, Horus the Child, the son of Isis and Osiris. It is a time of hope in the darkness of winter, for Horus is born with the destiny to overthrow the tyrant Set and reclaim his father's throne, thereby re-establishing order and justice in the Two Lands.

A long extract from one of the *Coffin Texts*, which constitutes a significant part of this rite, seems to emphasize the conception rather than the birth of Horus. It is probable that this extract is all that remains of an ancient sacred drama. It may be that originally the text would have contained an account of the birth too, but there is a lacuna at about the point where this occurs. It is unclear how much, if any, material describing the birth is missing. RO Faulkner thinks that the birth occurs where some lines are lost, but RT Rundle Clark locates it at the point where Isis says, 'Go up on earth, that I may give you praise,' though he attributes these words to Atum rather than Isis. At what seems to be the appropriate point we have therefore inserted the beautiful invocation of Horus from *The Book of the Dead*, so that the participants may experience the birth of the Divine Child within their own hearts.

'God of One Face' is a title of Horus, who is here identified with Thoth, Osiris and Nekhen. The 'divine Twin-gods' are Horus and Ra. Sebek is a crocodile god. Meht-urt is a sky goddess represented as a cow. The 'Releaser', a term which may also be translated as the 'Retreated One', refers to Ra, who, according to myth, has withdrawn from the world since the rebellion of mankind which was suppressed by Sekhmet. Isis has requested that Horus may also become a 'Releaser' or 'Retreated One' – possibly meaning a star.

The Birth of Horus

Cast the circle in the usual way and, if desired, call on Qebhsennuf in the East, Duamutef in the South, Imsety in the West and Hapi in the North for protection.

Two candles on the altar are unlit at start of rite. Incense is also unlit. The Priestess has a sistrum.

Shake sistrum.

Light the candles.

FIRST PARTICIPANT: The shining Eye of Horus cometh. The brilliant Eye of Horus cometh. It cometh in peace, it sendeth forth rays of light unto Ra in the horizon, and it destroyeth the powers of Set, according to the decree. It leadeth them on and it taketh possession of him, and its flame is kindled against him. Its flame cometh and goeth about, and bringeth adoration; it cometh and goeth about

heaven in the train of Ra upon the two hands of thy two sisters, O Ra. The Eye of Horus liveth, yea liveth.

Light the incense.

SECOND PARTICIPANT:
The fire is laid, the fire shines;
The incense is laid on the fire, the incense shines.
Your perfume comes to us, O Incense;
May our perfume come to you, O Incense:
Your perfume comes to us, you gods;
May our perfume come to you, you gods;
May we be with you, you gods;
May you be with us, you gods.
May we live with you, you gods;
May you live with us, you gods.
We love you, you gods;
May you love us, you gods.

Shake sistrum.

PRIEST: I come that I may greet you, you Mourner of Osiris, who conceal the Great One from the flood of ill; Mistress of thrones who makes a spirit of the Bull of the West, at seeing whom the Westerners rejoice; Mistress of All in the secret places ...

She of the papyrus plant whose milk is sweet.

She of vegetation which her lord divided ...

Mistress of the night who takes possession of the Two
Lands.

She who bent Set on account of her utterance.

She who cleared Horus's vision for him.

She who placed her lord in her embrace for herself ...

[Isis.]

FIRST PARTICIPANT: The lightning flash strikes, the gods are afraid, Isis wakes pregnant with the seed of her brother Osiris. She is uplifted, even she, the widow, and her heart is glad with the seed of her brother Osiris.

PRIESTESS AS ISIS: O you gods, I am Isis, the sister of Osiris, who wept for the father of the gods, even Osiris who judged the slaughterings of the Two Lands. His seed is within my womb, I have moulded the shape of the god within the egg as my son who is at the head of the Ennead. What he shall rule is this land, the heritage of his grandfather Geb, what he shall say is concerning his father, what he shall kill is Set the enemy of his father Osiris. Come, you gods, protect him within my womb, for he is known in your hearts. He is your lord, this god who is in his egg, blue-haired of form, lord of the gods, and great and beautiful are the vanes of the two blue plumes!

PRIEST AS ATUM: Oh! guard your heart, O woman!

PRIESTESS AS ISIS: How do *you* know? He is the god, lord and heir of the Ennead, who made you within the egg. I am Isis, one more spirit-like and august than the gods; the god is within this womb of mine and he is the seed of Osiris.

PRIEST AS ATUM: You are pregnant and you are hidden, O girl! You will give birth, being pregnant for the gods, seeing that he is the seed of Osiris. May that villain who slew his father not come, lest he break the egg in its early stages, for the Great-of-Magic will guard against him.

PRIESTESS AS ISIS: Hear this, you gods, which Atum, Lord of the Mansion of the Sacred Images, has said. He has decreed for me protection for my son within my womb, he has knit together an entourage about him within this womb of mine, for he knows that he is the heir of Osiris, and a guard over the Falcon who is in this womb of mine has been set by Atum, Lord of the gods. Go up on earth, that I may give you praise. The retainers of your father Osiris will serve you, I will make your name, for you have reached the horizon, having passed the battlements of the Mansion of Him whose name is hidden. Strength has gone up within my flesh, power has reached into my flesh!

Shake sistrum.

FIRST PARTICIPANT: Hail thou hawk who risest in heaven, thou lord of the goddess Meht-urt!

ALL: Strengthen thou me according as thou hast strengthened thyself, and show thyself upon earth, O thou that returnest and withdrawest thyself, and let thy will be done.

SECOND PARTICIPANT: Behold the god of One Face is with me.

PRIEST AS HORUS: I am the hawk which is within the shrine; and I open that which is upon the hangings thereof.

PRIESTESS: Behold Horus the son of Isis.

ALL: Behold Horus the son of Isis! Strengthen thou me according as thou hast strengthened thyself, and show thyself upon earth, O thou that returnest and withdrawest thyself, and let thy will be done.

FIRST PARTICIPANT AS THOTH: I am the hawk in the southern heaven, and I am Thoth in the northern heaven; I make peace with the raging fire and I bring Maat to him that loveth her.

PRIESTESS: Behold Thoth, even Thoth!

ALL: Strengthen thou me according as thou hast strengthened thyself, and show thyself upon earth, O thou that returnest and withdrawest thyself, and let thy will be done.

PRIEST: Behold the god of One Face is with me.

SECOND PARTICIPANT AS OSIRIS: I am the plant of the region where nothing sprouteth, and the blossom of the hidden horizon.

PRIESTESS: Behold Osiris, yea Osiris!

ALL: Strengthen thou me according as thou hast strengthened thyself, and show thyself upon earth, O thou that returnest and withdrawest thyself, and let thy will be done.

FIRST PARTICIPANT: Behold the god of One Face is with me.

PRIESTESS: Hail thou who standest upon thy legs, in thine hour ... Hail thou who art victorious upon thy legs, in thine hour, thou lord of the divine Twin-gods, who livest in the divine Twin-gods.

ALL: Strengthen thou me according as thou hast strengthened thyself, and show thyself upon earth, O thou that returnest and withdrawest thyself, and let thy will be done.

PRIESTESS: Behold the god of One Face is with me.

PRIEST: Hail thou Nekhen who art in thine egg, thou lord of the goddess Meht-urt.

ALL: Strengthen thou me according as thou hast strengthened thyself, and show thyself upon earth, O thou that returnest and withdrawest thyself, and let thy will be done.

FIRST AND SECOND PARTICIPANTS: Behold the god of One Face is with me.

PRIESTESS: The god Sebek hath stood up within his ground, and the goddess Neith hath stood up within her plantation.

ALL: O thou that returnest and withdrawest thyself, show thyself upon earth and let thy will be done.

PRIEST AND FIRST AND SECOND PARTICIPANTS: Behold the god of One Face is with me.

ALL: Strengthen thou me according as thou hast strengthened thyself, and show thyself upon earth, O thou that returnest and withdrawest thyself, and let thy will be done. Behold the god of One Face is with me.

PRIEST AS HORUS: See Horus, you gods! I am Horus, the Falcon who is on the battlements of the Mansion of Him whose name is hidden. My flight aloft has reached the horizon, I have overpassed the gods of the sky, I have made my position more prominent than the Primeval Ones. The Contender has not attained my first flight, my place is far from Set, the enemy of my father Osiris. I have used the roads of eternity to the dawn, I go up in my flight, and there is no god who can do what I have done ... I am Horus, born of Isis, whose protection was made within the egg; the fiery blast of your mouths does not attack me, and what you may say against me does not reach me, I am Horus, more distant of place than men or gods; I am Horus, son of Isis.

Shake sistrum.
Meditation.
Shake sistrum.

PRIESTESS AS ISIS: O Falcon, my son Horus, dwell in this land of your father Osiris in this your name of Falcon who is on the battlements of Him whose name is hidden. I ask that you shall be in the suite of Ra of the horizon in the prow of the primeval bark for ever and ever.

SECOND PARTICIPANT: Isis goes down to the Releaser who brings Horus, for Isis has asked that he may be the Releaser as the leader of eternity.

PRIEST: We give thanks to Isis, to Horus, to Thoth, to Osiris, to Atum, and to all the deities who have helped us in this rite.

If the Sons of Horus, Qebhsennuf, Duamutef, Imsety and Hapi, have been called on for protection, they should be thanked too and bid farewell, before dissolving the circle.
Shake sistrum.

SOURCES: *The Pyramid Texts*, Utterance 269, translation by RO Faulkner. *The Coffin Texts*, Spells 148, 828 and 993, translation by RO Faulkner. *The Book of the Dead*, Chapters 71 and 137B, translation by EA Wallis Budge.

Suppliers and Other Contacts

F or those who are new to Egyptian Paganism, it can be difficult to make contact with others worshipping Egyptian deities, and to obtain statuettes, altar equipment and other ritual implements. Because general Pagan organizations tend to be oriented towards Wicca, they may not be the best places to acquire information about the Egyptian Tradition.

For getting in touch with other devotees of Egyptian deities, the Fellowship of Isis is helpful. It has members in over 90 countries, so if you join, you may be able to make contact with someone near you.

Equipment such as candles, candlesticks, incense, cups, jars, bowls, incense holders and decorative boxes may be obtained from New Age outlets, gift shops and the gift sections of large department stores. Look for items of an art deco design (which is based on Egyptian design), or coloured black, turquoise or russet, or with a gilt finish, or decorated with a lotus motif: these will help to create an

Egyptian mood. Egyptian blends of incense are sometimes available as joss sticks, but if you cannot find these, frankincense is always suitable. (Incidentally, some people are adversely affected by incense smoke. A suitable alternative is to use essential oils on an aromatherapy burner. Kyphi and other Egyptian blends are available as oils.)

Egyptian-style greetings cards, pictures and posters, and common items such as ankhs, scarabs, Eye of Horus amulets, ornamental pyramids and sphinxes, are also often found in New Age shops. Look in your local business directory to see if there is one in your area.

Reproductions of Egyptian statuettes are sometimes attainable from museum shops. Museums which have Egyptian exhibits are likely to sell books on ancient Egypt, items of an Egyptian design, educational material for children, and Egyptian-oriented craft kits.

New Age and astrology magazines often carry advertisements by Pagan and occult suppliers. Such magazines may also have a section of small advertisements, including those from Pagan and occult organizations. It should be borne in mind that businesses supplying this sort of service are often very small, run by one or two people from their own homes, making the goods themselves in the garden shed or back bedroom. It is our experience that a few such businesses may occasionally close down suddenly, change address or otherwise be unreliable, so it is advisable to test the standard with a small order first. Be aware also that there may be a delay of several weeks if items have to be made especially for the individual customer. On the other hand, the people running these businesses are usually Pagan and can be friendly and helpful, often able to give advice or put enquirers in touch with another supplier if they themselves are unable to provide what is needed.

Listed below are a few addresses of organizations and businesses of which we have had personal experience, and which we have found to be reliable. It is also worth looking on the Internet for suitable contacts.

Fellowship of Isis, Clonegal Castle, Enniscorthy, Eire. Established in 1976 by Honourable Olivia Robertson and Reverend Lawrence and Pamela Durdin-Robertson, the FOI is an international organization for devotees of the Goddess. It is not primarily Egyptian, but because of the name it has attracted large numbers of devotees of Isis and other Egyptian deities. Many contacts, local groups, and several courses run by the groups. Membership free. Annual subscription for newsletter. Send International Reply Coupon with enquiry.

Lyceum of Isis Myrionymous, BM Box 1129, London WC1N 3XX. Right Reverend Doctor Jocelyn Almond offers a Fellowship of Isis Magi Degree course in 21 monthly parts by correspondence, with initiation and ordination for those who seek this. Send sae for information or six first-class stamps or International Reply Coupon for Introduction paper.

Temple of Khem, c/o Ignotus Press, BCM-Writer, 27 Old Gloucester Street, London WC1N 3XX. This mystery school offers a 13-month correspondence course in Egyptian magic, suitable for those who already have some experience of magic and Paganism. Send sae or International Reply Coupon for information.

The British Museum, Great Russell Street, London WC1B 3DG. Telephone 0207 323 8000. Minicom 0207 323 8920. Website [http://www.thebritishmuseum.ac.uk] The British Museum has one of the best Egyptian collections in the world. The museum bookshop has a large range of books on ancient Egypt, including academic books which are difficult to obtain elsewhere. There is also an impressive gift shop where some Egyptian-inspired items are available, including statuettes and craft kits.

British Museum Company Mail Order. For catalogues, information or to order, **telephone 0207 323 1234. Fax 0207 436 7315.**

Sacred Source, PO Box 163, Crozet, VA 22932, USA. Telephone: 434 823 1515. Fax: 434 823 7665. e-mail [spirit@sacredsource.com] Website [http://www.sacred-source.com] Full colour catalogue available. Extraordinarily large range of hand-painted statuettes of Pagan deities of the world's cultures, made from clay from the sacred River Ganges by Indian craftworkers. A selection of Egyptian figures includes some less well-known deities as well as the major ones. Of special note is a beautiful large winged Isis. Also, books, cards and novelties. (Prices are reasonable, but you should take into account extra costs of postage and customs duty when ordering from abroad.)

Sacred Moon, 27 Wyle Cop, Shrewsbury, Shropshire SY1 1XB. Telephone: 01743 352829. Send £1.50 or six International Reply Coupons for catalogue. General Pagan catalogue which includes some excellent Egyptian items. Small and medium-sized statuettes in simulated black stone, hand-finished, made in Egypt, including Anubis and Thoth with human bodies, and Bast as a cat. Silver pendants (ankhs and some deities), incense, and non-Egyptian items (tapes, CDs, candles, oils, wands, crystal balls, scrying mirrors).

Tamera Today, PO Box 56, Penzance, Cornwall TR20 9YP. Website [http://www.tameratoday.co.uk] Specializes in items relating to ancient Egypt, supplying books, jewellery, figurines of deities, incenses, oils, altar cloths and much more. Free catalogue on request.

Contacting the Authors

We are pleased to receive enquiries concerning any aspect of this book and Egyptian Paganism in general. Please write to us at **BM Box 1129, London WC1N, 3XX, England**, enclosing a stamp or International Reply Coupon, or see
http://mysik.freeserve.com/lyceum2/index.html

Glossary

Abydos Greek name for Abtu. Cult centre of Osiris.

Aker An earth god in the form of a lion with two forequarters.

Akert/Aukert The underworld.

Ament/Amenti/Amentet The underworld, realm of the dead, identified with goddess Hathor.

Amit A fire goddess.

Ammut (Pronounced 'Amoot'.) A goddess in the form of a composite animal who devours the unrighteous dead.

Amun (Pronounced 'Amoon'.) Creator god, the 'hidden one', often identified with Ra.

An A form of the sun god.

Anes bandlet A bandlet of red linen.

Antes Meaning unknown.

Annu On, Heliopolis.

An-rut-f 'The place where nothing grows' – a region of the underworld.

Anubis (Pronounced with emphasis on second syllable.) Greek name for Anpu. Dog or jackal god of embalming, guide of souls. Son of Nephthys and Osiris (or Set).

Apep The giant serpent of chaos, enemy of Ra.

Asyut (Pronounced 'As-yoot'.) Ancient town of Middle Egypt.

Atet/Matet boat (Pronounced 'Ah-tet'/'Mah-tet'.) The sun god's boat from midnight to midday.

Aten (Pronounced 'Ah-ten'.) The deified sun disc.

Atmu A god of the primeval waters.

Atum (Pronounced 'Atoom'.) The Creator, the 'complete one', often identified with Ra.

Bah Heron god of plenty. A deity identified with Ra.

Ben-ben A pyramidal stone representing the Primeval Mound on which the Creator stood at the creation of the world, or alternatively the petrified semen of the sun god. The original ben-ben was probably a meteorite.

Bull of Djedu/Bull of Nedit/Bull of the West Titles of Osiris.

Children of impotent rebellion Chaos demons, enemies of Ra, followers of Apep.

Conclaves Two assemblies of the gods, for Upper Egypt and for Lower Egypt.

Coptos Capital of the fifth nome, one of two principal cult centres of Min.

Djed (Pronounced 'Jed'.) A ceremonial pillar, possibly representing a tree. Can symbolize the backbone of the risen Osiris, used as amulet.

Djedu (Pronounced 'Jeddu'.) Busiris, cult centre of Osiris.

Djendru-bark (Pronounced 'Jendroo'.) A deified sacred boat.

Duamutef (Pronounced 'Dwa-moo-tef' with emphasis on the second syllable.) A Son of Horus, depicted with a jackal's or dog's head. (May be regarded as god of elemental fire.) Sometimes female.

Edjo A name of the goddess Wadjet, identified with Hathor.

Ennead (Pronounced 'En-ee-ad' with emphasis on the first syllable.) Greek term for the pesedjet – a group of nine deities worshipped at Heliopolis. An idea copied by other cult centres.

Epiphi The month from May 15 to June 13.

Eye of Horus/Eye of Ra The sun, identified with goddesses Hathor and Sekhmet. The Eye of Horus is often conceived of as his left eye, the moon. (See **Utchat/Wedjat**.)

Field of Rushes Idyllic region of the afterlife realm, in heaven.

Four Sons of Horus Four deities which guard the bodily organs of the dead and represent the four elements and cardinal points. They are Qebhsennuf, Duamutef, Imsety and Hapi.

Geb (Pronounced 'Geeb' with a hard G.) God of the earth, son of Shu and Tefnut, brother and husband of Nut, father of Osiris, Horus the Elder, Set, Isis and Nephthys.

Gehesty The place where Osiris was murdered.

God of One Face A title of Horus.

Hamemet Celestial beings who may have been or may become human.

Hapi (Pronounced 'Haahpy'.) God of the Nile, depicted as a man with pendulous breasts.

Hapi/Hapy (Pronounced 'Haahpy'.) A Son of Horus, depicted with an ape's or baboon's head. (May be regarded as god of elemental earth.)

Harakhti (Emphasis is on the second syllable.) 'Horus of the horizon', the constellation of Leo and a form of the sun god.

Har-Sopd Horus identified with Sopdu, the falcon god of the eastern Delta.

Hathor (Pronounced 'Haythor' or 'Hat-hor'.) Sky goddess, daughter of Ra, depicted as a cow or cow-eared woman. Goddess of love and beauty.

Hau-nebut (Pronounced 'Hor-neboot'.) The Isles.

Heka Magic, sometimes personified as a god.

Henti period Sixty years.

Heru-hekennu A member of the Great Triad of Bubastis, offspring of Osiris and Bast, depicted as a hawk-headed man.

Heru-khenti-an-maati 'Horus dweller in darkness', the Blind Horus, i.e. when neither the sun nor the moon is visible.

Heru-khuti 'Horus of the Two Horizons'. Horus, especially as the god of the rising sun (and Horus or Osiris as the constellation of Orion).

Het-benbenet 'Mansion of the Pyramidion', capstone of a pyramid – the dwelling of the sun god.

Het-ka-Ptah 'The House of Ptah's ka', Memphis.

Hetepet 'Lady of offerings', or 'Lady of peace', consort of Atum.

Horus Greek name for Hor, Har or Heru. The sun god in the form of a falcon. Horus the Elder (Haroeris) is the brother of Osiris, Set, Isis and Nephthys. Horus the Younger or Child (Harpocrates or Harsiese) is the son of Isis and Osiris. These two Horuses are often conflated.

Hor-em-Akhet 'Horus in the horizon', the Sphinx, a form of the sun god.

Hunnu The sun god.

Iasu (Pronounced 'Yassoo'.) A heavenly region.

Imsety (Pronounced with emphasis on the second syllable.) A Son of Horus. (May be regarded as god of elemental water.)

Ipu Panopolis, capital of the ninth nome of Upper Egypt, one of two principal cult centres of Min.

Isis Greek name for Aset. Great Mother goddess of wisdom, compassion and magic. Daughter of Nut and Geb (or Ra, or Thoth), sister of Horus the Elder, Set and Nephthys, sister and wife of Osiris, mother of Horus the Younger. Identified with Sothis/Sirius.

Khepera Creator god of the rising sun. A form of Ra, depicted as a scarab beetle.

Kher-aha Religious centre south of Cairo.

Khnum (Pronounced 'Kuh-noom'.) Creator god, depicted with a ram's head, who moulds humans on his potter's wheel.

Khu   A spirit.

Lake of Sehseh/Lake of Testes   Regions of the sky or
   underworld.

Maat   Goddess of justice, truth and order, daughter of Ra.

Mansion of the Prince in On   Palace of divine justice in
   Heliopolis.

Medja-land   The eastern deserts of Nubia.

Meht-urt/Meh-urt/Mekhwert/Mehet-Weret   A sky goddess,
   Neith-Hathor in the form of a cow.

Menth/Mont   Falcon-headed war god of Thebes.

Mert   The Two Songstress-goddesses. (Isis and Nephthys.)

Mounds of Horus/Mounds of Set   Regions of the sky or
   underworld.

Mut   (Pronounced 'Moot'.) Mother goddess in the form of a vulture.

Nak   A name of Apep, the chaos serpent.

Neb-er-Tcher   'Lord of All', the Creator, identified with Ra.

Nedit   'Where he was cast down', the place where Osiris was
   murdered.

Neith   (Pronounced 'Neet'.) War-like Creator goddess of Sais.

Nekhbet   Vulture goddess, symbol of Lower Egypt on pharaonic
   crown.

Nekhen   An ancient city in Upper Egypt. A falcon deity identified
   with Horus.

Nephthys Greek name for Nebet-Het. Goddess of twilight, death and grief. Daughter of Nut and Geb, sister of Osiris, Horus the Elder and Isis, sister and wife of Set, mother of Anubis.

Nepra/Neper A god of the grain.

Neter (Pronounced 'neeter' or 'neecher'.) A divine principle or emanation. A god (Plural – **neteru**.)

Neterkhert (Pronounced 'Neeterkert' or 'Neecherkert'.) 'Divine under place'. An inner spiritual or psychic realm.

Nu The father god of the Nun, primeval waters.

Nun (Pronounced 'Noon'.) The primeval waters of chaos before Creation.

Nut/Nuit (Pronounced 'Noot' or 'Noo-it'.) Goddess of the night sky, daughter of Shu and Tefnut, sister and wife of Geb, mother of Osiris, Horus the Elder, Set, Isis and Nephthys.

Ogdoad (Pronounced 'Og-doh-ad'.) Group of eight primeval deities worshipped at Hermopolis.

On (Pronounced 'Own.') Heliopolis, cult centre of Ra.

Osiris (Pronounced with emphasis on the second syllable.) Greek name for Asar. God of the underworld and resurrection, identified with fertile earth, corn, Nile in flood, and constellation of Orion. Son of Nut and Geb, brother of Horus the Elder, Set and Nephthys, brother and husband of Isis, father of Horus the Younger and Anubis.

Parehaqa-Kheperu (Pronounced 'Para-hacka-Kepperoo'.) A form of the sun god, spouse of Sekhmet-Bast-Ra.

Pashakasa (Pronounced 'Pasha-kahsa'.) A child of Sekhmet-Bast-Ra.

Pelican Mother goddess of the dead who prophesies a safe passage through the underworld.

Per-nu National shrine of the Delta under protection of Wadjet.

Per-wer National shrine of Upper Egypt.

Pert Winter, the growing season.

Ptah (Pronounced 'Ta'.) Creator god of Memphis, architect of the universe, husband of Sekhmet.

Ptah-Seker/Ptah-Seker-Tem (Pronounced 'Ta-Seker-Tem'.) The Creator Ptah identified with gods of death and the setting sun.

Qebhsennuf (Pronounced 'Kebsnoof'.) A Son of Horus, depicted with a falcon's head. (May be regarded as god of elemental air.)

Ra The Creator, the sun god, depicted as a falcon or falcon-headed man.

Ra-Harmachis (Pronounced 'Rah-Harm-ackis', emphasis on 'ack'.) Ra identified with Hor-em-Akhet, the Sphinx.

Ra-er-Neheh 'Ra the everlasting'.

Red Crown Deshret, the pharaonic crown of the North or Lower Egypt.

Releaser The 'Retreated One' – Ra after his withdrawal from the earth. Horus as a star.

Renenutet Fertility goddess of the harvest, depicted with a serpent's head.

Rostau 'The entrance of the ways', called the 'place more noble than any place', the plateau of Giza.

Sebek A crocodile god.

Sekhem 'Power', a title of Ra and other deities.

Sekhmet Destroyer form of Hathor as the Eye of Ra, the sun, depicted as a lioness-headed woman. Wife of Ptah.

Sekhmet-Bast-Ra A compound male-female deity, combining Sekhmet with her gentle cat form, Bast, and the sun god Ra. Perhaps a form of Mut.

Sekhtet/Semktet boat The sun god's boat from midday to midnight.

Seksut (Pronounced 'Seksoot'.) Meaning unknown.

Sektet The High Priest at Heliopolis.

Senut (Pronounced 'Senoot'.) A sanctuary of the god Min in the ninth nome of Upper Egypt.

Set/Seth God of chaos, storms, destruction and the desert. Son of Nut and Geb, brother of Osiris, Horus the Elder and Isis, brother and husband of Nephthys. (Possibly father of Anubis.)

Shen-a-sek A sea.

Shesmetet (Pronounced 'Shes-meet-tet'.) 'Lady of Malachite', a title of Hathor.

Shu God of the atmosphere. Son of Ra, brother and husband of Tefnut, father of Nut and Geb.

Sia God of the intellect and the perceptive mind.

Sistrum-player Priest of Hathor or her son.

Sokar/Seker A falcon god of the dead, identified with Osiris. His image was borne on a ceremonial boat on a sledge at his festival.

Sothis Greek name for Sopdet. The goddess Isis as the star Sirius.

Souls of Pe Falcon deities representing ancient idealized ancestors.

Stela Greek word for a slab or pillar (often a gravestone), usually bearing an inscription. (Plural – **stelae**.)

Suten-henen Capital of Heracleopolis, a nome (district) of Egypt.

Tamt The universal god.

Ta-tchesert The Sacred Land.

Ta-thenen/Tatenen Creator god in the form of a ram. Personification of the Primeval Mound.

Tefnut (Pronounced 'Tefnoot'.) Goddess of moisture, depicted as a lioness-headed woman. Daughter of Ra, sister and wife of Shu, mother of Nut and Geb.

Tem/Temu God of the setting sun, depicted as a ram-headed man. Identified with Ra.

Tet A female symbol associated with Isis, in the form of a bow. Used as an amulet.

Thigh The constellation of the Great Bear.

Thinite Nome A district of Upper Egypt of which the capital was a cult centre of Osiris.

Thoth (Pronounced to rhyme with 'both'.) Greek name for Tehuti/Djehuty. A moon god of wisdom, learning and magic, inventor of writing, keeper of records. The Mind of the Creator, depicted as an ibis-headed man.

Tuat (Pronounced 'Dwat'.) The underworld, or region of the sky near the horizon.

Twin gods Horus and Ra, or Osiris and Ra.

Two Ladies of Dep   The uraeus goddess Wadjet of Upper Egypt and the vulture goddess Nekhbet of Lower Egypt as emblems on the pharaonic crown.

Un-nefer   'The good being', a title of Osiris.

Unti   A god holding stars who walks before the solar bark.

Uraeus   (Greek. Plural – **uraei**.) The sacred serpent, a cobra.

Ureret/wereret crown   The White Crown of the South or Upper Egypt.

Utchat/Wedjat   The 'healthy eye' or left eye of Horus, being the moon, which was stolen by Set (when the moon waned) and restored by Thoth.

Utchatet   The Sacred Eye.

Utent   A region in the south of Egypt.

Wadjet   Uraeus (cobra) goddess of Upper Egypt, appearing as emblem on pharaonic crown.

Wag festival   Held on the eighteenth day of the first month – 5 August.

Was staff   The animal-headed sceptre of power carried by some deities.

Wedjat   See 'Utchat'.

Wepwawet   A dog, jackal or wolf deity similar to Anubis.

Wereret   See 'ureret'.

White Crown   Pharaonic crown of the South or Upper Egypt.

Bibliography

Baring, Anne, and Cashford, Jules (1993) *The Myth of the Goddess*, London, Arcana.

Bauval, Robert, and Gilbert, Adrian (1994) *The Orion Mystery*, London, Heinemann.

Bauval, Robert, and Hancock, Graham (1997) *Keeper of Genesis*, London, Mandarin.

Buckland, Raymond (1987) *Buckland's Complete Book of Witchcraft*, St Paul, Minnesota, Llewellyn.

Budge, EA Wallis (1969) [1904] *The Gods of the Egyptians* (2 volumes), New York, Dover.

—— (1989) *The Book of the Dead*, London, Arcana.

—— (1991) [1899] *Egyptian Magic*, New York, Wings Books.

—— (1997a) [1900] *Egyptian Religion*, Secaucus, New Jersey, Citadel Press.

—— (1997b) [1914] *An Introduction to Ancient Egyptian Literature,* New York, Dover.

Clark, RT Rundle (1978) *Myth and Symbol in Ancient Egypt,* London, Thames and Hudson.

Crowley, Aleister (1973) *Magick,* London, Routledge & Kegan Paul.

Durdin-Robertson, Lawrence (1990) *The Year of the Goddess,* Wellingborough, Aquarius.

Farrar, Janet, and Farrar, Stewart (1981) *Eight Sabbats for Witches,* London, Robert Hale.

—— (1984) *The Witches' Way,* London, Robert Hale.

Faulkner, RO (1969) *The Ancient Egyptian Pyramid Texts,* Warminster, Aris and Phillips.

—— (1973) *The Ancient Egyptian Coffin Texts* (3 volumes), Warminster, Aris and Phillips.

—— (1985) *The Book of the Dead,* London, British Museum Press.

Fortune, Dion (1987a) *Applied Magic and Aspects of Occultism,* London, Aquarian Press.

—— (1987b) *Esoteric Orders and their Work and the Training and Work of the Initiate,* London, Aquarian Press.

—— (1987c) *Sane Occultism and Practical Occultism in Daily Life,* London, Aquarian Press.

González-Wippler, Migene (1988) *The Complete Book of Spells, Ceremonies and Magic,* St Paul, Minnesota, Llewellyn.

Hart, George (1986) *A Dictionary of Egyptian Gods and Goddesses,* London, Routledge and Kegan Paul.

Hornung, Erik (1992) *Idea into Image: Essays on Ancient Egyptian Thought,* New York, Timken.

Ions, Veronica (1997) *Egyptian Mythology*, London, Chancellor Press.

Jacq, Christian (1985) *Egyptian Magic*, Warminster, Aris and Phillips.

—— (1997) *Fascinating Hieroglyphics*, New York, Sterling Publishing.

Kaster, Joseph (1995) *The Wisdom of Ancient Egypt: Writings from the Time of the Pharaohs*, London, Michael O'Mara.

Knight, Gareth (1979) *The Practice of Ritual Magic*, Wellingborough, Aquarian Press.

Kraig, Donald Michael (1988) *Modern Magick: Eleven Lessons in the High Magickal Arts*, St Paul, Minnesota, Llewellyn.

Lamy, Lucie (1981) *Egyptian Mysteries: New Light on Ancient Knowledge*, London, Thames and Hudson.

Lichtheim, Miriam (1975) *Ancient Egyptian Literature* (3 volumes), Berkeley, University of California Press.

Lurker, Manfred (1982) *An Illustrated Dictionary of the Gods and Symbols of Ancient Egypt*, London, Thames and Hudson.

Meeks, Dimitri, and Farvard-Meeks, Christine (1997) *Daily Life of the Egyptian Gods*, London, John Murray.

Naydler, Jeremy (1996) *Temple of the Cosmos: The Egyptian Experience of the Sacred*, Rochester, Vermont, Inner Traditions.

Paddon, Peter (1985) *The Book of the Veil*, Freshfields, Chieveley, Capall Bann.

—— (1996) *Through the Veil*, Freshfields, Chieveley, Capall Bann.

O'Regan, Vivienne (1992) *The Pillar of Isis*, London, Aquarian Press.

Reed, Ellen Cannon (1992) *Invocation of the Gods*, St Paul, Minnesota, Llewellyn.

Regula, deTraci (1995) *The Mysteries of Isis*, St Paul, Minnesota, Llewellyn.

Index